S0-AFQ-476

A HISTORY OF
PAN-AFRICAN REVOLT

A HISTORY OF
PAN-AFRICAN REVOLT

C. L. R. JAMES

Drum and Spear Press
Washington, D.C.

Second edition, revised, 1969.

© Copyright, 1969, by C. L. R. James.

All rights reserved.

Library of Congress catalogue card number 79-107493

Printed in the United States of America.

CONTENTS

INTRODUCTION

This book is a double landmark. It is the first publication of Drum and Spear Press. In these days when black people throughout the world are clamouring for self-knowledge, Drum and Spear Press has recognized the need in servicing this rising concern.

For the author, C. L. R. James, the volume represents work that has spanned a period of thirty-one years. The bulk of this work first appeared in a monograph series called FACT in 1938. The author's wisdom is time-tested. Changes, for clarity's sake, are less than a dozen lines.

James's own experience, in the midst of Negro toils and struggles, embraces the past and present. He was a part of those profound forces who saw independence come to Ghana in 1957. He was a close observer of the events in Kenya marking the rise of "Mau Mau". In the Caribbean of course, he spoke, wrote and organized as a partisan to the West Indian resistance struggle. In the United States, James is known to two generations of black men who have chosen rebellion and resistance as an alternative course to living under American domination.

Today, C. L. R. James is still close to the international movement of black men who seek seriously to oppose oppression and to pursue a course of meaningful self-development. James has become a great source of wisdom and counsel to youth in the Resistance Movement. Still inspired by the new events of the struggle he has taken great interest in the course to revolution chosen by Tanzania following that country's Arusha Declaration.

C. L. R. James is probably the greatest chronicler of the Negro's long standing international revolt against slavery and imperialistic control. In 1938 he finished a history of the Haitian revolution entitled *The Black Jacobins*. The present revised work embraces the whole scope of revolts which have broken out in the Pan-African world since the time of the San Domingo Revolution. To the original manuscript which appeared in FACT James has added the important events of the last two decades which continue to reshape the relation of black people to Imperialism.

I am glad that this volume of C. L. R. James' studies of Black Rebellion is coming back into publication. I hope to see more of his work widely distributed and read. Also, I hope that Drum and Spear Press will continue to bring into circulation works of such significance.

Marvin Holloway,

Center for Black Education

Washington, D.C.
October, 1969

Chapter 1

San Domingo

The history of the Negro in his relation to European civilization falls into two divisions, the Negro in Africa and the Negro in America and the West Indies. Up to the 'eighties of the last century, only one-tenth of Africa was in the hands of Europeans. Until that time, therefore, it is the attempt of the Negro in the Western World to free himself from his burdens which has political significance in Western history. In the last quarter of the nineteenth century European civilization turned again to Africa, this time not for slaves to work the plantations of America but for actual control of territory and population. Today* the position of Africans in Africa is one of the major problems of contemporary politics. An attempt is made here to give some account and analysis of Negro revolts through the centuries; in the days of slavery; in Africa during the last half-century; and in America and the West Indies to-day.

It is impossible in this space to deal with the slave-trade and slavery; the same consideration has made it necessary to omit accounts of the early revolts in the West Indies and the incessant guerilla warfare carried on in all the islands by the maroons (or runaway slaves) against their former

* Today = 1938

1

masters. Negroes have continually revolted and once in Dutch Guiana the revolting slaves held almost the entire colony for months. But in the eighteenth century the greatest colony in the West Indies was French San Domingo (now Haiti) and there took place the most famous of all Negro revolts. It forms a useful starting point.

1789 is a landmark in the history of Negro revolt in the West Indies. The only successful Negro revolt, the only successful slave revolt in history, had its roots in the French Revolution, and without the French Revolution its success would have been impossible.

During the eighteenth century French San Domingo developed a fabulous prosperity and by 1789 was taking 40,000 slaves a year. In 1789 the total foreign trade of Britain was twenty-seven million pounds, of which the colonial trade accounted for only five million pounds. The total foreign trade of France was seventeen million pounds, of which San Domingo alone was responsible for eleven millions. The French bourgeoisie of the maritime towns, Marseilles, Bordeaux, Nantes, owed most of their wealth to the slave-trade. 'Sad irony of human history', comments Jaurès, 'the fortunes created at Bordeaux, at Nantes, by the slave-trade gave to the bourgeoisie that pride which needed liberty and contributed to human emancipation.' But the colonial system of the eighteenth century ordained that whatever manufactured goods the colonists needed could be bought only in France.

They could sell their produce only to France. The goods were to be transported only in French ships. Colonial planters and the Home Government were thus in bitter and constant conflict, the very conflict which had resulted in the American War of Independence. The American colonists gained their freedom in 1783, and in less than five years the British attitude to the slave-trade changed.

Previous to 1783 they had been the most successful practitioners of the slave-trade in the world. But now not only was America gone, but it was British ships which were supplying a large proportion of the 40,000 slaves a year which were the basis of San Domingo's prosperity. The trade of San Domingo almost doubled between 1783 and 1789. The British West Indian colonies were in comparison poor, and with the loss of America, were of diminishing importance. The monopoly of the West Indian sugar planters galled the rising industrial bourgeoisie, potential free-traders. Adam Smith and Arthur Young, economists of the coming industrial age, condemned the expensiveness of slave labour. India offered the example of a country where the labourer cost only a penny a day, did not have to be bought, and did not brand his master as a slave-owner. In 1787 the Abolitionist Society was formed and the British Government, which only a few years before had threatened to sack a Governor of Jamaica if he tampered with the slave-trade in any shape or form, now changed its mind. If the slave-trade was brought to a sudden close, San Domingo would be ruined. The British islands would lose nothing, for they had as many slaves as they seemed likely to need. The abolitionists it is true worked very hard, and Clarkson, for instance, was a very honest and sincere man. Many people were moved by their propaganda. But that a considerable and influential section of British men of business thought that the slave-trade was not only a blot on the national name but a growing hole in the national pocket, was the point that mattered. The evidence for this is given in detail in the writer's *Black Jacobins* published in 1938 with a revised edition in 1963.

The Abolition Society was formed in 1787. France at that time was stirring with the revolution, and the French humanitarians formed a parallel society, "The Friends of the Negro." They preached the abolition not only of the slave-trade but of slavery as well, and Brissot, Mirabeau, Condorcet, Robespierre, many of the great names of the revolution, were among the members. They ignored or minimized the fact that, unlike Britain, two-thirds of France's overseas trade was bound up with the traffic. Wilberforce and Clarkson encouraged them, gave the society money, and did active propaganda in France. This was the position in Europe when the French Revolution began.

San Domingo possessed at that time 500,000 slaves, and only 30,000 Mulattoes and about the same number of whites. But the slave-owners of San Domingo at once embraced the revolution, and as each section interpreted liberty, equality and fraternity to suit itself, civil war was soon raging between them. Some of the rich whites, especially those who owed debts to French merchants, wanted to follow the example of America and virtually rule themselves. The Mulattoes wanted to be rid of their disabilities, the poor whites wanted to become masters and officials like the rich whites. These classes fought fiercely with one another. The white colonists lynched and murdered Mulattoes for daring to claim equality. But the whites themselves were divided into royalists and revolutionaries. The French revolutionary legislatures first of all evaded the question of Mulatto rights, then gave some of the Mulattoes rights, then took the rights away again. Mulattoes and whites fought, and under the stress of necessity began to arm their slaves. The news from France, the slogans of liberty, equality and fraternity, the political excitement in San Domingo, the civil war between rich whites, poor whites and Mulattoes, it was these things which after two years awoke the sleeping slaves to revolution. By July, 1791, in the thickly populated North they were planning a rising.

The slaves worked on the land, and, like revolutionary peasants everywhere, they aimed at the extermination of their masters. But, working and living together in gangs of hundreds on the huge sugar-factories which covered the North Plain, they were closer to a modern proletariat than any group of workers in existence at that time, and the rising was, therefore, a thoroughly prepared and organized mass movement.

On a night in August a tropical storm raged, with lightning and gusts of wind and heavy showers of rain. Carrying torches to light their way, the leaders of the revolt met in an open space in the thick forests of the Morne Rouge, a mountain overlooking Cap François, the largest town. There Boukman, the leader, after Voodoo incantations and the sucking of the blood of a stuck pig, gave the last instructions.

That very night they began. Each slave-gang murdered its masters and burnt the plantation to the ground. The slaves destroyed tirelessly. They knew that as long as those plantations stood, their lot would be to labour on them until they dropped. They violated all the women who fell into their hands, often on the bodies of their still bleeding husbands, fathers and brothers. But they did not maintain this vengeful spirit for long. As the revolution gained territory they spared many of the men, women and children whom they surprised on plantations. To prisoners of war alone they remained merciless. They tore out their flesh with red-hot pincers, they roasted them on slow fires, they sawed a carpenter between his boards. Yet on the whole, they never approached in their tortures the savageries to which they themselves had been subjected.

The white planters refused to take the slave revolt seriously. They continued to intrigue against the Mulattoes and to threaten the French Government. But as the chaos grew, the rich royalists swallowed their colour prejudice and united with the Mulattoes against the revolutionary planters. Meanwhile the insurrection prospered, until a few weeks after it began there were about a hundred thousand revolting slaves divided into large bands. The leaders were Jean-François and Biassou, and Toussaint Louverture joined them a month after the revolt began. He was forty-six, first his master's coachman and afterwards, owing to his intelligence, placed in charge of the livestock on the estate, a post usually held by a white man. He had a smattering of education, but he could not write correct French, and usually spoke creole i.e. the local French patois.

Baffled in their first spring at the city, these leaders did not know what to do, and when the French Government sent Commissioners who boasted of the armed forces (quite imaginary) which were on their way, the Negro leaders sought to betray their followers. They wrote to the Commissioners promising that in return for the freedom of a few hundred they would co-operate in leading the others back into slavery and would join in hunting down the recalcitrant. Toussaint, in charge of the negotiations, reduced the offer from 400 to 60. The French Commissioners gladly accepted, but the white planters with great scorn refused. Toussaint therefore gave up hopes of even a treacherous solution and began to train a small band of soldiers from among the hordes.

The French legislature was by this time under the leadership of Brissot and the Girondins. These managed to persuade the colonial interests that it was to their advantage to give all rights to the Mulattoes, and in April 1792, this became law. But Brissot, doughty propagandist for abolition before he came to power, now would not go a step further than rights for Mulattoes. Far from abolishing slavery, he and his government despatched a force to crush the slave revolt. These troops landed in San Domingo, but before they could begin the attack, events had occurred in Paris which altered the whole course of the French Revolution, and with it, the black revolution in San Domingo.

On August 10, 1792, the Paris masses, tired of the equivocations and indecision of the Parliamentarians, stormed the Tuileries and dragged the Bourbons off the throne. A wave of enthusiasm for liberty swept over France and from indifference to slavery at the beginning of the revolution, revolutionary France now hated no section of the aristocracy so much as the colonial whites, 'the aristocrats of the skin.' In San Domingo the news of August 10 so split the slaveowners that the civil war between them which had ended began again. Every conflict among the slave-owners was a source of added strength to the slaves.

By February 1793 war had broken out between revolu-

tionary France and England and Spain. The Spaniards in
Spanish San Domingo from the start had helped the slaves
against the French. Now they offered them a formal alliance
and the slaves trooped over to join Spain. Whether France
was a republic or reactionary monarchy, made no difference
to the colonial slave if each was prepared to keep him in
slavery. Toussaint Louverture went with the others but he
secretly offered to the French the services of his trained band
if they would abolish slavery. They refused. He made a
similar offer to the Spanish commander who likewise refused.
Toussaint decided to stay where he was and watch develop-
ments. Sonthonax, the French Commissioner, at his wits'
end, threatened by Britain and Spain and increasingly deserted by the French blacks, abolished slavery as his last
chance of gaining some support. His manoeuvre failed.
Toussaint remained with the Spaniards and won most of the
North Province for them. For the planters, abolition was the
last straw and they offered the colony to Pitt, who despatched
an expedition from Europe to capture the French colonies in
the West Indies. The British carried all before them, and by
June 1794 over two-thirds of San Domingo and almost every
French island of importance were in the hands of the British.
The rest seemed only a matter of days.

But meanwhile the revolution had been rising in France.
Before the end of 1793 Brissot had been swept out of power.
Robespierre and the Mountain ruled and led the revolution

against its enemies at home and abroad. By this time all revolutionary France had embraced the cause of the slaves, many refusing even to touch coffee as being drenched with the blood of their own human kind. On February 4, 1794, the Convention abolished slavery without a debate. 'The English are beaten', shouted Danton. 'Pitt and his plots are riddled.' The great master of revolutionary tactics had seen far. The British fleet prevented assistance going to the hard-pressed coloured revolution but the decree of abolition would throw the blacks wholeheartedly on the side of the French. Toussaint joined the French at once, and slaughtered his Spanish allies, white and black, of yesterday; while in Martinique, Guadeloupe, and the other French colonies, the black slaves, singing the *Ça Ira* and the *Marseillaise* and dressed in the colours of the Republic, began to drive the British out of the French islands, and then carried the war into British territory.

Spain made peace in 1795, and by 1799 the British had been driven out of San Domingo and most of the French colonies by Negro slaves and Mulattoes. Fortescue, the Tory historian of the British army, gives a vivid account of this colossal disaster. Britain lost 100,000 men in the West Indies in these four years, two and a half times as many as Wellington lost in the whole of the Peninsular War. Fever took a heavy toll, but Toussaint Louverture, and Rigaud, a Mulatto, in San Domingo; and Victor Hugues, a Mulatto, in Martinique and the smaller islands, won one of the most important victories in the French revolutionary wars. Aided by the fever, they, in Fortescue's phrase, 'practically destroyed the British army.' For six years Britain was tied up in the West Indies, and to quote Fortescue once more, if Britain played so insignificant a part in the attack on revolutionary France in Europe during the first six years of the war, the answer is to be found in 'the two fatal words, San Domingo.' The part played by the blacks in the success of the great French Revolution has never received adequate recognition. The revolution in Europe will neglect coloured workers at its peril.

With the British driven out, Louverture occupied a powerful position. He was Commander-in-Chief, appointed by the French Government, of a French army, with white officers under him. But as soon as the British were driven out, the French started to intrigue against him. They engineered a quarrel between himself and Rigaud, the Mulatto, whence was fought a bitter civil war. Toussaint was victorious, then brought Spanish San Domingo under his control. He established a strong government over the whole island, drew up a constitution which made him First Consul for life, and gave San Domingo 'dominion status'; concentrating all the power in his own hands, he governed. In eighteen months he had restored a colony, devastated by years of civil war, to two-thirds of its former prosperity. He was a despot, confining his

labourers to the plantations and brooking no interference
with his will under harsh penalties. But he protected the
labourers from the injustice of their former owners. He saw
that they were paid their wages. He established free trade
and religious toleration, abolished racial discrimination, tried
to lay the foundations of an educational system, sent young
Mulattoes and Negroes to France to be educated so as to
return and be able to govern. He treated the whites with
exceptional consideration and courtesy, so much so that the
black labourers began to lose confidence in him. Too confi-
dent of his influence over the blacks, he sacrificed his popu-
larity to please the French.

But the political situation in France had changed for the
worse. The revolution had stabilized itself under Bonaparte.
And Bonaparte sought to restore slavery. He sent an expedition under his brother-in-law Leclerc which finally amounted
to nearly 60,000 men. Toussaint vacillated at first, then
fought and finally came to terms. Captured by a trick he was
sent to France, and died in an Alpine prison. But as soon as
Bonaparte's plans for the restoration of slavery and all the
discriminations of the old regime became known, the population, which had been partially deceived by Leclerc's false
proclamations, revolted. Dessalines, one of Toussaint's lieutenants, had by this time seen what Toussaint never saw, that
only independence could guarantee freedom. The Mulattoes,
who had previously supported Bonaparte, joined the blacks,

and together they fought a desperate war of independence. To win they had almost to destroy the island. France, from casualties in battle and fever, suffered the loss of over 50,000 men. The cruelties practised by the French during the last stages of the civil war exceeded in barbarism the worst of the old slavery days. Dessalines, uncultured and lacking Toussaint's genius, led his people with a ruthlessness quite equal to that of the French.

The attitude of the whites towards changes in the San Domingo regime throws a valuable light on race prejudice. Before the revolution Negroes were so despised that white women undressed before them as one undresses to-day before a dog or a cat. Ten years after, when former slaves were now ruling the country, most of the whites accepted the new regime, fraternized with the ex-slave generals and dined at their tables; while the white women, members of some of the proudest families of the French aristocracy, threw themselves recklessly at the black dictator, sent him locks of hair, keepsakes, passionate letters, etc. To the labouring Negroes, however, they showed as much of their old hostility as they dared. When the Leclerc expedition came, the whites rushed to join it, and took a leading part in the gladiatorial shows where dogs ate living Negroes, etc. But when they saw that Leclerc's expedition was doomed to defeat, they disentangled themselves from it and turned again to the blacks. Dessalines, the new dictator, declared the island independent, but promised them their properties. This was enough for them. When the French commanders were about to evacuate the island they offered the white colonists places on the boats. The colonists refused, being quite content to continue living under blacks who were no longer French even in allegiance: the San Domingo blacks gave their island its old Carib name, Hayti, to emphasize the break with France.

But the British and the Americans, themselves the greatest slave-holders in the world, were all for the victory of the blacks in order to drive out the French. All through Leclerc's campaign the British and American newspapers cursed the French and praised Toussaint and the blacks. That Frenchmen should remain in the island did not suit them. While Dessalines, who hated the whites for their accumulated treacheries, wanted to kill as many as possible, Christophe and Clairveaux, his two trusted lieutenants, disapproved, and the great bulk of the people wanted no more bloodshed. But Cathcart, an English agent in San Domingo, told Dessalines that the British would neither trade with him nor accord him their protection unless every Frenchman were killed. Not long after the French were massacred. M. Camille Guy tells the story and gives his original sources in pamphlet No. 3 of the *Bulletin de géographie,* published in Paris in 1898. There too he gives details of the presents that were sent to Dessalines for his coronation from London in a British cruiser and from America. Needless to say, in most books on this subject, black Dessalines bears the sole responsibility for this massacre.

The success of the San Domingo blacks killed the West Indian slave-trade and slavery. France hoped for many years that she would regain the colony. The Haytians let her know that they would resist to the last man and burn everything to the ground. France therefore resigned herself to the loss and with the removal of San Domingo from the West Indian trade, abolition of the slave-trade in 1807 and of slavery in 1834 followed. The English planters fought hard but history was against them. The revolution in France in 1848, during its short-lived span of success, abolished slavery in the French colonies.

The San Domingo revolution is the only successful Negro revolt, and therefore the reasons for that success must be noted. First the blacks themselves fought magnificently and glowing tributes have been paid to them by their opponents. But many had fought well before and have fought well since. They were fortunate in that they had had time to organize themselves as soldiers. And this was due to the fact that they not only received inspiration from the revolution in France but between 1794 and 1797 had active support from revolutionary France. Such supplies and reinforcements as did actually arrive were comparatively small, but were directed towards assisting and not retarding the slave revolution. This was the decisive factor. The international situation also helped them. But the conflict between Britain and France, then between France on the one hand and Spain on the other was also the result of the revolution. During the last campaign, at a very critical moment, the declaration of war between France and Britain, after the short interval which followed the Treaty of Amiens, made the victory of the San Domingo blacks inevitable. But the blacks manoeuvred with great skill. The Spaniards, and in the later stages after their defeat, the British, both offered terms to the blacks with the secret intention of turning upon them afterwards and restoring slavery. Maitland, the British general, say so very clearly in his letter to the Foreign Secretary, Dundas, dated December 26, 1798, and preserved in the Public Record Office. But Toussaint never compromised himself with the British. While taking from them as much assistance as was convenient, he refused any entangling alliances. He thus made the most skilful use of imperialist contradictions when revolutionary France, crushed, was no longer able to assist him.

There remains to be noted a certain aspect of the struggle which though derivative is yet of extreme importance. During the revolutionary period the blacks fought under the slogans of liberty and equality. They embraced the revolutionary doctrine, they thought in republican terms. The result was that these slaves, lacking education, half-savage, and degraded in their slavery as only centuries of slavery can degrade, achieved a liberality in social aspiration and an elevation of political thought equivalent to anything similar that took place in France. Hundreds of Toussaint's letters, proclamations, etc., are preserved, some in the national archives in France, others in San Domingo. Papers of contemporary blacks and Mulattoes also exist. Christophe and Dessalines, who shared the leadership with Toussaint, were quite illiterate, slaves sprung from the ranks. But they and their fellow officers not only acted but spoke and dictated like highly-trained modern revolutionaries.

Some examples should be given. All the blacks did not join the French. Some remained with the Spanish rulers of Spanish San Domingo. The leader of these, full of racial pride, rejected the overtures of the French and told Laveaux, the French Commander, that he would only believe in his pretended equality when he saw Monsieur Laveaux and gentlemen of his quality giving their daughters in marriage to Negroes. But the blacks who were republican had the utmost scorn for the blacks who were royalist. Witness the following proclamation in reply to overtures made on behalf of the Spanish authorities by the blacks who supported royalism.

> We are republicans and, in consequence, free by natural right. It can only be Kings whose very name expresses what is most vile and low, who dared to arrogate the right of reducing to slavery men made like themselves, whom nature had made free.

The King of Spain furnishes you abundantly with arms
and ammunition. Use them to tighten your chains. . . .
As for us, we have no need for more than stones and sticks
to make you dance the Carmagnole. . . .
You have received commissions and you have guarantees.
Guard your liveries and your parchments. One day they
will serve you as the fastidious titles of our former aristocrats served them. If the King of the French who drags
his misery from court to court has need of slaves to assist
him in his magnificence, let him go seek it among other
Kings who count as many slaves as they have subjects.

When Toussaint Louverture began to suspect in 1797
that the French Government was now the representative of
forces which might ultimately aim at the restoration of
slavery, he addressed to them a letter which seems to come
straight from the pen of Mirabeau, Danton or Robespierre,
instead of from a slave who dictated in the local patois and
then had his thoughts written and rewritten until his secre-
taries had achieved the form which he desired.

Do they think that men who have been able to enjoy the
blessing of liberty will calmly see it snatched away? They
supported their chains only so long as they did not know
any condition of life more happy than that of slavery. But
to-day when they have left it, if they had a thousand lives
they would sacrifice them all rather than be forced into
slavery again. But no, the same hand which has broken
our chains will not enslave us anew. France will not revoke
her principles, she will not withdraw from us the greatest
of her benefits. She will protect us from all our enemies;

she will not permit her sublime morality to be perverted, those principles which do her most honour to be destroyed, her most beautiful achievement to be degraded, her Decree of the 16th Pluviôse which so honours humanity to be revoked. *But if, to re-establish slavery in San Domingo, this was done, then I declare to you it would be to attempt the impossible: we have known how to face dangers to obtain our liberty, we shall know how to brave death to maintain it.* (Italics his own.)

This, Citizen Directors, is the morale of the people of San Domingo, those are the principles that they transmit to you by me.

My own you know. It is sufficient to renew, my hand in yours, the oath that I have made, to cease to live before gratitude dies in my heart, before I cease to be faithful to France and to my duty, before the god of liberty is profaned and sullied by the liberticides, before they can snatch from my hands that sword, those arms, which France confided to me "for the defence of its rights and those of humanity, for the triumph of liberty and equality."

Race prejudice was rampant before the revolution and blacks and Mulattoes hated each other as much as did the blacks and whites. Yet by 1799 when the civil war was about to begin between the blacks of the North and West and the Mulattoes of the South, a civil war based on the different social interests of the two classes, Rigaud the Mulatto leader, instead of emphasizing the difference in colour as Mulattoes always did before the revolution, now defended himself with moving passion against the conception that he was hostile

to Toussaint, the Commander-in-Chief, because Toussaint
was a Negro.

> Indeed, if I had reached the stage where I would not wish
> to obey a black, if I had the stupid presumption to believe
> that I am above such obedience, on what grounds could I
> claim obedience from the whites? What a grievous ex-
> ample would I be giving to those placed under my orders?
> Besides, is there so great a difference between the colour
> of the Commander-in-Chief and mine? Is it a tint of
> colour, more or less dark, which instils principles of phi-
> losophy or gives merit to an individual? . . . I have conse-
> crated my life to the defence of the blacks. From the
> beginning of the revolution I have braved all for the cause
> of liberty. I have not betrayed my principles and I shall
> never do so. Besides, I am too much a believer in the
> Rights of Man to think that there is one colour in nature
> superior to another. I know a man only as a man.

The revolution under the encouragement of the French
revolutionaries seemed to have created a new nation. The
great tragedy of San Domingo was that as the revolution in
France retreated before reaction, the old slave-owners re-
gained influence and harassed the exhausted blacks.

Chapter 2

The Old United States

The revolts in the United States follow the same line as those in the West Indies before 1789, constant ill-organized uprisings which are always crushed with comparative ease.

A typical revolt was that which took place at Stono, a plantation some twenty miles to the West of Carolina, in September 1739. A few score of slaves killed the two guards of a magazine, armed themselves and set out for the Edisto river. Other Negroes joined them, they marched with colours displayed, drums beating, shouting for liberty, and killing and burning all in their path. They killed about twenty-five whites, but spared one who was a good man and kind to his slaves. After some miles of this destruction they stopped to rest, but were surprised by their white owners who had followed in pursuit. They fought bravely, but they were defeated, and most of them were either shot in battle, hanged, or gibbeted alive. That is the theme on which the variations were played in state after state in America as in island after island in the West Indies. The slaves gained nothing by these revolts. No attempt is made to treat them more kindly. Instead revolts are savagely repressed and the severity of slave legislation increased.

Yet these American revolts between 1670 and 1860 follow certain laws. This of 1739 was one of a series which took
place in South Carolina between 1737 and 1740, a period of
grave economic difficulties. There is imperialist intrigue at
work. Spain still had colonies in America and the Spaniards
were encouraging these American slaves to rebel. Many of
the Negroes had been captured in Angola, and being Catholic, were attracted to the Spaniards. When the revolting
Negroes set out for the Edisto river, they intended to follow
it to its mouth, which was in Spanish territory. Finally the
Negroes outnumbered the whites four to one in this state.
Yet despite these favourable circumstances the revolt seems
to have neglected the thousands of slaves who, it may be
presumed, were not unwilling to join. While their masters
lived in constant terror, the Negroes themselves seemed unconscious of their revolutionary potentialities when organized on an extensive scale.

The San Domingo revolution and its success dominated
the minds of Negroes in the West Indies and America for the
next generation. In America, where the slaves had periodically revolted from the very beginning of slavery, San Domingo inspired a series of fresh revolts during the succeeding
twenty years. Documented accounts of these American
slave revolts have appeared in the United States. In 1795
a revolt in Louisiana failed to take place owing to a quarrel
as to the method. But this revolt is notable because an im-

portant feature now appears which seems to have been the direct result of the revolutionary ferment of the age: there were whites in alliance with the Negroes from the very beginning. Five years afterwards, in 1800, there took place the well-known revolt headed by the Negro slave Gabriel, in Virginia. The white authorities, fortunately for them, heard about it before the uprising actually began and were thus able to take precautions. About a thousand slaves, armed with clubs and swords which they had been making since the last harvest, gathered six miles away from the town of Richmond. But a tremendous storm flooded the rivers, tore down bridges and made it impossible to conduct military operations. The revolt ended as always in failure and bloody suppression. Yet Gabriel and his followers were slave revolutionaries above the average. They intended to spare Frenchmen because the Frenchmen were associated in their minds with liberty, equality and fraternity. They were also going to spare Quakers and Methodists because these were consistently opposed to slavery. They confidently expected the poorer whites to join them. After the fore-doomed defeat, Gabriel was captured, tried and executed. It is not known how many Negroes were concerned, but the numbers suggested varied between 2,000 and 10,000.

Despite the accidents which overtook this revolt at its beginning, it is impossible to see what other result but defeat awaited it. It had no support among powerful revolutionary elements in the country. It had no support abroad. Similar failures awaited the plots in Virginia and North Carolina in 1801–2. For these, however, we have clear evidence that the poor whites of the districts had definitely allied themselves with the Negroes. This is the recruiting speech of one of the revolting Negroes: 'I have taken it on myself to let the country be at liberty, this lies upon my mind for a long time. Mind men I have told you a great deal I have joined with both black and white which is the common men or poor white people, Mulattoes will join with me to help free the country, although they are free already. I have got 8 or 10 white men to lead me in the fight on the magazine, they will be before me and hand out guns, powder, pistols, shot and other things that will answer the purpose . . . black men I mean to lose my life in this if they will take it."

There were risings in 1811 and again in 1816, but even as late as 1822 in Virginia, one Denmark Vesey, a free Negro, attempted to lead a revolt which was partially inspired by San Domingo. Vesey based his attempt on his readings of the Bible, but he also had the San Domingo revolution in mind, for he wrote to the rulers of Hayti, telling them of his plans and asking for aid. Despite his religious outlook, or because of it, all who opposed the rising were to be killed. The numbers involved were said to have been between 6,000 and 9,000, and some of his supporters came from as far away as eighty miles. The insurrection was betrayed, probably by that mischievous type—the house-slave who was kindly treated by his master and wore his cast-off clothes.

The last important American revolt was Nat Turner's, born out of the anti-slavery agitation which was to end in the abolition of slavery in the British colonies. Mexico abolished slavery in 1829 and in this period, right through the West Indies and Spanish America, there was slave revolt after slave revolt. Turner's revolt was not very wide in scope. An intelligent and gifted man, he took his inspiration from the Bible. In February 1831 about 70 Negroes, some of them mounted, covered an area of about 20 miles and killed about 60 women and children. They were ultimately defeated by hundreds of state troops. Turner was caught and hanged.

So far Turner's revolt was commonplace. But this revolt had an effect out of all proportion to its size. Though there are reports of slave conspiracies and of plots all over the Southern states for the next thirty years, nothing on a large scale seems to have been attempted. On the other hand at the time of the Turner revolt the Southern slave owners realized that the unrest 'was not confined to the slaves.' Henceforward the fear of unity between the blacks and the poor whites drove the South to treat with great severity any opposition to slavery in the South from whatever source it came. A rigid censorship was instituted. In the years before the American Civil War the turmoil among the slaves was widespread all over the South. Their chance came, however, not from the poor whites of the South but from the economic and political necessities of the Northern whites.

Chapter 3

The Civil War

Before we consider the course of emancipation in America, let us see what the Negroes were to be emancipated from. In 1860, little more than seventy-five years ago, Negro slavery was still widespread in the Southern states of America. We know what slavery was like during the eighteenth century. It had not changed much in the last half of the nineteenth.

Here is a case that reads as if it came straight from San Domingo, Barbados or British Guiana in 1749. '. . . The Negro was tied to a tree and whipped with switches. When Souther became fatigued with the labour of whipping, he called upon a Negro man of his and made him "cob" Sam with a single. He also made a Negro woman of his help to "cob" him. And, after "cobbing" and whipping, he applied fire to the body of his slave, about his back, belly and private parts. He then caused him to be washed down with hot water in which pods of *red pepper* had been steeped. The Negro was also tied to a log, and to the bed-post, with ropes, which choked him, and he was kicked and stamped upon by Souther. This sort of punishment was continued and repeated until the Negro died under its affliction.' The records

of the time tell the same tale of burnings, mutilations, etc.,
as in the West Indies 150 years before.

Every slave-owner did not spend every hour of the day
beating and torturing his slaves. But few of his neighbours
cared if he did, and if he tortured them, it was done so frequently that it occasioned no surprise in those who saw it.
In this respect 1860 was not very different from 1660. Glad-
stone and *The Times* both supported the slave-owners
against the North in the American Civil War.

In this very period, Governor Eyre of Jamaica, without
the slightest justification, authorized a murderous persecution of Negroes who had revolted under great provocation
and had behaved with great moderation. Maroons were
called in, who dashed out the brains of children and ripped
open pregnant women; while the more civilized Provost-
Marshal Ramsay shot victims with his own hand and flogged
victims until their flesh bespattered the ground. Nearly 500
Negroes were killed and thousands of Negroes were whipped,
sometimes with a cat in the strings of which piano-wire was
interwoven; as many as two hundred lashes each were administered. Britain was divided, Carlyle leading the defence
of Eyre, who was retired on pension. Coming as it did just
at the time of the American Civil War, this incident is related
here, so that the cruelty of Americans to their slaves might
be seen in reasonable perspective.

Obviously the conscience of mankind or growing enlightenment was not going to abolish Negro slavery in America. These forces in the heart of man had not abolished slavery for 250 years. Why should they suddenly be potent in 1850?

First of all, as we have seen, the Negro was no docile animal. He revolted continuously. By 1850 he had changed his tactics. For over a generation before the outbreak of the Civil War, the bolder slaves of the South sought freedom by flight to the North, whose economic structure had no need of slavery. In the South, the mountaineers of North Carolina, Kentucky and Tennessee had no need of slaves. They formed anti-slavery societies, and Christian and Liberal revolutionaries assisted fugitive slaves to escape. These and some bold Negroes organized the famous Underground Railway to assist escaping slaves. By various special routes slaves were conducted from the South to the Northern states, where they were free. Thousands of blacks gained their freedom in this way. Bravest and most famous of these underground guides was the Negro, Harriet Tubman. Born a slave, she escaped, but rifle in hand she devoted her life to assisting others to actual freedom by means of the Underground. The Southern owners offered a reward of 40,000 dollars for her capture, but she used to penetrate into the very heart of the South in order to achieve her aims. Not only slaves but free Negroes took part in all this agitation and organization. When John Brown made his famous raid there were Negroes with him, some of whom lost their lives in the fighting, and others at the hands of Southern law. The agitation of the abolitionists, the sensational escapes by the Underground Railway, the ferment among the Negroes, all helped to focus public attention on slavery. But long before the Civil War the great issues at stake were becoming clear.

The South had dominated the Federal Legislation for more than half-a-century, but with the increasing industrial expansion of the North, that domination was now in danger. Both North and South were expanding westward. Should the new states be based on slavery as the South wanted or on free capitalism as the North wanted? This was not a moral question. Victory here meant increasing control of the legislature by the victors. The moment the North were strong enough they decreed that there was to be no further extension of slave-territory. Nothing else remained for the South but war. Had the Southerners won, their reactionary method of production and the backward civilization based upon it would have dominated the United States. No wonder Karl Marx hailed the Civil War as the greatest event of the age. He was not concerned with the morality or immorality of slavery. What he could see so early was the grandeur of the civilization which lay before the States with the victory of the North. Thus if the Civil War resulted in the abolition of slavery it was not fought for the benefit of the slaves.

Yet Negro slavery seemed the very basis of American

capitalism. Slavery made cotton king; cotton became the very life food of British industries, it built up New England factories. This accounts for not merely the support given to the South by Conservatives but even by certain British Liberals. The protagonists had no illusions. Lincoln once told a Massachusetts audience cheerfully, 'I have heard you have abolitionists here. We have a few in Illinois, and we shot one the other day.' Lincoln said openly that to save the Union he would free all the slaves, or free some, or free none.

What we are really witnessing here is not that sudden change in the conscience of mankind so beloved of romantic and reactionary historians, but the climax of a gradual transformation of world economy. Where formerly landed property had dominated, the French Revolution marks the beginning of the social and political domination of the industrial bourgeoisie. It began in the French Revolution, in Britain its outstanding dates are the Reform Bill of 1832 and the Repeal of the Corn Laws in 1846, and it reached its culmination with the Civil War in America. The process worked itself out blindly and irrationally. In territories like San Domingo and later Brazil, where new and rich lands cried out for cultivation, the slave remained profitable for years. But we can see to-day that once capitalism had begun to throw off feudal shackles, slavery was doomed. The millions of slaves were not only ignorant and backward, with a low productivity of labour. Their potential consumption as free men widened the scope of the market. Thus the San Domingo revolution, the abolition of the slave-trade in 1807, the emancipation of the slaves in 1833, and emancipation during the Civil War in America, all these events are but component parts of a single historic process. However confused, dishonest, selfish, idealistic or sincere, might be the minds of the abolitionists, they were in the last analysis the agents of the economic necessities of the new age, translated into social and political, sometimes, even, religious terms.

Lincoln long maintained his attitude. It was the pressure of war which forced him to accept emancipation. The South were using Negroes to build fortifications, roads, etc., all the important labour of their armies. Where at first he feared a slave revolt which would weaken his political position in the North, he now saw the necessity of at least using slaves for labour purposes. Refugees poured over to the Northern forces and Lincoln tried to get some of them despatched to Africa, to Hayti and other territories outside America. He was at that time considering a scheme of gradual abolition based upon compensation.

But the Negro refugees were establishing themselves in the army as capable teamsters, mechanics, and general workers. They were industrious and loyal. The South was proving more difficult to conquer than had at first been thought, and the Negroes would have to be used as soldiers. In 1862 Congress declared that after January 1, 1863, all slaves in rebel territory were free. Northern generals were urging Lincoln to enlist Negroes, and one had already taken the step on his own initiative. The South formed corps of free Negroes which were fighting in its army. Thus Lincoln's objections were finally overborne by the necessity of events. Before the end of 1865 four Negro regiments were in the field and at the end of the war, three years afterwards, 178,875 Negroes had been enrolled in the Northern army. Seventy-five commissions were given, but the Negroes were commanded chiefly by white men. They were discriminated against, being treated as less than the equals of whites. Two regiments refused to accept their pay until it was made equal to that of white men, and one sergeant was court-martialled and shot because he made his company stack arms before the captain's hut as a protest against discrimination. White troops often used them for fatigue duty. This unfair treatment affected the morale of the blacks, who were often sullen and insubordinate. But of their military quality there was never any question. They defeated some of the crack Southern troops, men who had formerly owned them. Surgeon Seth Rogers said of his soldiers that braver men never lived, and Colonel T. W. Higginson declared that 'it would have been madness to attempt with the bravest white troops what he successfully accomplished with the black': the white troops were not fighting for freedom. Brave as were these blacks, there was nothing naïve about them. 'They met death cooly, bravely; nor rashly did they expose themselves, but all were steady and obedient to orders.' Lincoln himself admitted that but for the assistance given by the Negroes, the North might have lost. He spoke more wisely than he knew. Negro scholarship in America has conducted investigations which tend to show that not only the Negro soldiers but the Negroes left behind in the South played a decisive part in the outcome. In the first years of the war the Southern blacks took the side of their masters. They knew them, they did not know the North, and as both were for the maintenance of slavery the difference between them was of no importance. But after the proclamation of emancipation, the news spread and it is claimed that there took place a sort of general strike, an immense sabotage, which helped to bring the South to its knees. Slavery degrades, but under the shock of great events like a revolution, slaves of centuries seem able to conduct themselves with the bravery and discipline of men who have been free a thousand years.

The American blacks were far more indebted to the political conflicts between North and South America for their freedom than the San Domingo blacks had been to the French Revolution. They were only four million, a minority, even in the South. They were tied indissolubly to America. What was now to become of them?

The Negroes themselves knew what they wanted—the land—and had they been strong enough to take it, or had the Northern capitalists the wisdom to give it to them, the possibilities opened up both for the Negro and American capitalism would have been immense. The bourgeois revolution against feudalism is only economically complete when the peasants have the land. It was so in France in 1789 and in Russia in 1917. Peasants today are politically alert as never before.

The Negroes tried to take the land. They had fought with an instinctive confidence that it was going to be theirs, so much so that much of the idleness and discontent in certain areas after the Civil War could be traced to the fact that they had not got what they expected. In certain areas they actually seized the land and refused to return it. The Negro soldiers and the militia were trained to arms, they and their allies secured large quantities of ammunition, and in the latter part of 1865 the South lived in fear of a slave insurrection. The proposal was actually made to oppose the return of confiscated property and substitute instead a scheme for dividing the estates of the leading rebels into forty-acre plots for each freed man. The rest would be sold to pay off the national debt and fifty dollars would be given to each homestead as a start. Revolutionary as these proposals were, yet nine-tenths of the population of the South would have been untouched. But Parliament, though busy expropriating the farmers of the West and even the South for the benefit of the railroad and mining companies, would not touch Southern

property for the benefit of the Negroes. It would have meant
the creation of a body of peasant proprietors for whom co-
operative and similar schemes would have been comparatively easy, it would have resulted in a great extension of the
internal 'market,' and the Negro question would never have
been the problem that it is to-day in America. This revolution could easily have been accomplished in the early days
after the Civil War. The Southerners were too cowed to
resist, the sporadic efforts of the Negroes only needed co-
ordination. Why was the opportunity missed? First because
the peasants in a revolution have to seize the land. Only the
Jacobins, as late as 1793, ratified the seizure in France. The
Kerensky government in Russia could go no further than an
elaborate land law, and the peasants had to wait for the
Bolsheviks to encourage and legalize the seizure. Only a
revolution in which the poor were the driving force would
have held out its hand to the blacks and made common cause
of its own objectives and land for the blacks. There was no
such revolution in America. What the dominant American
bourgeoisie did, however, is as revealing of the true nature
of American race prejudice as the behaviour of the San
Domingo whites during the black revolution. The war had
divided the Northern bourgeoisie into the small men on the
one hand and on the other, the bankers, the magnates of iron
and steel and the railways, linking themselves into great
corporations. Monopoly capitalism was on its way. But it

was as yet small. In a new country its control of propaganda, organs of publicity, etc., was not sufficient to ensure its control of elections. The small capitalists would outnumber the big capitalists and gain control of the government. Writing in the *American Mercury* of April 1938, a Southerner has shown that the huge patriarchal estates of the South are a tenacious legend with no foundation in fact. Most of the Southern slave-owners were farmers on a not very large scale. There was also a small capitalist class growing in the South. A combination between these and their brethren in the North would be fatal to the monopolists. By illegally excluding representatives of the Southern States from the legislature, the big bourgeoisie passed legislation to ensure their predominance and enfranchised the Negroes in order to use these votes against their white rivals in the South. They then despatched special agents, the carpet-baggers, to pose as the friends of the Negro and to manipulate the Negro vote in their favour.

Thus the North did not allow race prejudice against the Negro to impede its wishes, accepted the fact that he was needed to help hold the South in control, and co-operated politically with him. The Southern states were offered the choice of military government or universal manhood suffrage 'without regard to colour, race or previous condition of servitude.' They were thus trapped either way. Some of the states accepted the Negro voter, others refused, among them

Virginia, Georgia and Texas. Between 1868 and 1872 certain states were governed by whites and blacks, many of the blacks being newly-emancipated slaves.

The idea that the Negroes dominated is wholly false. Only 23 Negroes served in Congress from 1868 to 1895. Many Negro state officials were illiterate; in certain state legislatures more than half the Negro members could scarcely read or write. Yet there were among them many capable men. There is no evidence to prove that they were more than usually corrupt or rapacious. The Northerners who entered these Southern governments and plundered them were potent sources of corruption. The black officials naturally sided with Northerners against the old slave-owners. When in a few years the Southern states were restored to Southern control, in nearly every state the white officers in control of the funds defaulted. But no exposure was made of this. In another generation, Northern monopoly capitalism had America in its grasp. It left the Negro to his fate, and the South turned on him. Landless, his Northern collaborators gone, he was whipped back to an existence bordering on servitude.

Yet despite the inevitable ignorance and backwardness, the few years during which the Negroes were associated with the government of certain Southern states marked the high watermark of progressive legislation in the South. Little publicity is given to the things they helped to do. 'They obeyed the Constitution and annulled the bonds of states, counties and cities which were issued to carry on the War of Rebellion and maintain armies in the field against the Union. They instituted a public school system in the realm where public schools had been unknown. They opened the ballot-box and jury-box to thousands of white men who had been debarred from them by lack of earthly possessions. They introduced Home Rule in the South. They abolished the whipping-post, the branding-iron, the stocks, and other barbarous forms of punishment which, up to that time, prevailed. They reduced capital felonies from about twenty to two or three. In an age of extravagance, they were extravagant in the sums appropriated for public works. In all that time no man's right of person was invaded under the forms of law. Every Democrat's life, home, fireside and business were safe. No man obstructed any white man's way to the ballot-box, interfered with his freedom or boycotted him on account of his political faith.' It was the policy of a people poor and backward seeking to establish a community where all, black and white, could live in amity and freedom. It deserves to be remembered.

Chapter 4

Revolts in Africa

For four centuries the African in Africa had had to suffer from the raids of the slave dealers and the dislocation of African civilization which had been caused thereby. America continued with the slave-trade until the end of the Civil War, but whereas in 1789 San Domingo alone was taking 40,000 slaves a year, between 1808 and 1860 the Southern states of North America took only 200,000. Other nations of Europe and the Arabs on the East coast continued the trade. Actual colonies, however, were comparatively few in Africa. There was, of course, Cape Colony and the districts beyond, and colonies in West Africa which were on the whole little more than trading stations. In the middle of the nineteenth century Disraeli referred to colonies as damned millstones around the necks of the British people. As we have said it is unlikely that more than one-tenth of Africa was in European hands. But in the 'eighties began the intensive rivalry of European imperialisms for colonies as the sources of raw materials, for markets and spheres of influence. By the end of the nineteenth century, less than one-tenth of Africa remained in the hands of Africans themselves. This rapid change could not fail to produce a series of revolts, which have never ceased.

Before we consider the actual revolts, it is necessary to see, briefly, what the Negro is revolting against. European colonization is broadly speaking of two types, the first, as in South Africa, the two Rhodesias and Kenya, where it is possible for Europeans to settle and remain; the second in British West Africa, where the European is for the most part official and trader, does not look upon the colony as his home and does not settle there in large numbers.

In areas like the Union of South Africa, the Rhodesias and Kenya, the white settlers have to force the native to leave his own work and interests in order to labour for them in mine or plantation. The method they adopt is to tax him by means of a poll tax. The Negro, though perhaps quite comfortably placed according to his own wishes and needs, must have money to pay this tax, which compels him therefore to seek employment with European masters, on whatever conditions these choose to lay down. Hence the wages of fourpence a day in Kenya and 15 shillings a month in the copper mines of Rhodesia. The Europeans also take the best land and herd the natives in areas which are not only difficult to cultivate but too small for their most elementary needs. In the Union of South Africa, for instance, about 2,000,000 whites own about eighty per cent. of the land, while over 6,000,000 natives own ten per cent. The rest is Crown land, that is to say, at the disposal of the white government. Obviously this state of affairs can only be maintained by a social and political regime based on terror.

The natives are made to carry passes which they must produce on request; a pass if they are out later than nine o'clock, a pass to show that their tax has been paid, a pass from their employer, finger-prints for identification—in the Union of South Africa there are a dozen passes of one kind or another which the Negro may have to carry. A Negro who has a profession is given an exemption pass which absolves him from the necessity of carrying these other passes. But any native policeman is able to ask him for this exemption pass, and arrest him on the spot if it is not produced at once. Negroes, whatever their status, whatever their appearance, are debarred from frequenting all public places of business or entertainment frequented by whites. In places like the post office, there are two counters, one for whites and one for blacks.

What does the native get in return? After four hundred years of European occupation, there are not half-a-dozen native doctors in South Africa. Over three-quarters of the native population is almost entirely without education. The education supplied to the rest is officially admitted to be of the poorest quality. Far from making a gradual, if slow, political progress, the natives of the Cape have recently been deprived of the franchise, a relic of more liberal days. They are debarred by law from being even skilled labourers, as tyrannical and demoralizing a piece of legislation as has been passed in any country during the last hundred years.

In the mines they receive one-eighth of the wages of the white miner. In ancient territories like the Union of South Africa, or in more modern areas as Rhodesia and Kenya, the method is exactly the same, with slight local variations. While politicians in Britain speak of trusteeship, South African white leaders and officials in Rhodesia and Kenya periodically state quite unequivocally that Africa is to be run for the benefit of the whites and the Negro must make up his mind to know his place and keep it.

In West Africa the situation is somewhat different. There, over large areas, the Negroes were guaranteed their land by law, at a time when it seemed unlikely that Europeans would ever need it. European capital, of course, dominates. But the racial discrimination is not nearly so acute as in the South and in the East of Africa, and the conflict between the Negroes and their rulers is more strictly economic and political than it is in the Cape or Kenya.

French Equatorial Africa and the Belgian Congo form two areas to some degree different from those described above. In a French colony, a Negro who by education or military service becomes a French citizen, is given all privileges, and is governed by the laws which apply to white men. He can become a high official in the government service, or a general in the French army. During the war Petain's Chief of Staff at Verdun was a Negro. Commandant Avenol, who was in charge of the air defence of Paris from 1914 to 1918 with ten thousand men under him, including British and white American aviators, was a Martinique Negro. At the present moment the Governor of Guadeloupe is a black man. These men, it is true, are from the old West Indian colonies. But there are Africans in the service, and it is admitted that promotion is open to them on practically the same terms as whites. There have been Africans, deputies in the Chamber, who have become Cabinet Ministers. After the war the French issued a serious warning to Americans in Paris who tried to introduce American race prejudice, and it is note-worthy that these Americans who cannot tolerate the sight of a Negro in an American restaurant, learnt in Paris to admit him and his white girl friends into an American bar: Briand told them that he would close down the bar if they didn't. This is a valuable feature of French civilization and disposes of many illusions, carefully cultivated in America and Britain, about Negro incapacity and racial incompatibility. But im-perialism remains imperialism. During the last twenty years the population of French Congo has declined by more than six millions, and the French have as black a record in Africa as any other imperialist nation.

In the Belgian Congo the Negro has certain priviliges; for example, he is allowed to occupy important posts on the railways, which is forbidden to him in South Africa. Thus Negroes run trains to the border of the Belgian colonies where South African whites take them over. Yet the Belgian attitude is less liberal than the French. No African who has spent more than six months abroad is allowed to return to the Congo, and the severity of the forced labour regulations is such that when the company which owns the sugar plantations of Moabeke built a railway, almost the entire male population of the district was worked to death. This is in no way exceptional. French and Belgians have an evil reputation in the Congo for cold-blooded cruelty. As in the days of slavery in the West Indian colonies, the European colonizing nations claim superiority to each other. But an African in Eritrea is no worse off under Italian Fascism than an African in the Congo under democratic Belgium, or a Rhodesian copper miner.

The Old Colonies

Let us begin with revolts in one of the oldest colonies on the West Coast, Sierra Leone. The Negroes in the actual colony are some of the most advanced in education and should be grouped with those of the West Indies rather than with those in Central or Eastern Africa. Freetown, the capital, for instance, was until recent years a municipality. The hinterland is, however, a protectorate where the less developed Africans are governed by the method of indirect rule.

At the end of the last century there were two Negro communities, one with its own press, barristers-at-law, doctors and other intelligentsia, and on the other hand the natives in the interior, the new Africa and the old. These two communities were divided. Those with generations of British education had an outlook similar to that of the majority of Negroes in the West Indies: they regarded the African tribes as barbarous and uncivilized. The African tribes looked upon these Europeanized blacks as black white men. In 1898 a revolt burst in the protectorate. The natives resented the paying of the poll tax and the Mendi, a famous fighting tribe, had a special grievance of their own: they objected to corporal punishment. So much did they oppose it, that they would not send their children to the missionary schools where the missionaries sometimes beat them. The tribes completely wiped out some battalions of West Indian blacks who were sent against them, and it is claimed by Negroes who were in Sierra Leone at the time that certain white battalions were also completely destroyed. The great massacres of government soldiers took place at Sherbro and Mofeno. The revolt was of course put down, many hundreds of natives being killed. The insurgents killed not only white and black soldiers and every missionary they could put their hands on, but also certain of the Europeanized blacks as well. They looked upon all of these as members of one exploiting, arrogant group. The war, however, has marked the beginning of a change.

The conflict of capital and labour is intensified by the fact that capital is usually white and labour black; this in a continent where the whites have always sought to justify their economic exploitation and social privilege by the mere fact of difference of colour. The class conflict, bitter enough in countries where the population is homogeneous in colour, has an added bitterness in Africa, which has been strengthened by the growth of nationalism among the post-war intelligentsia. The politically conscious minority increasingly realize that their future is with the developing Africans rather than with the European traders. Further, they are Africans in Africa—not the descendants of Africans, as in the West Indies. The result is a growing solidarity between the blacks, chiefly workers in the colony and the more untutored Africans in the protectorate. Black politicians in the colony attribute the ill-feeling in 1898 to white propaganda aimed at dividing potential allies, and they have common ground in that they are Negroes in a continent where to be black is to be inferior. It is against this background that we must see more recent movements in Sierra Leone and Gambia.

In 1919 there was a railway strike in Sierra Leone. The railway workers attempted to get other workers to join with them and were joined by over 2,000 police striking for higher

wages. In 1926 there was another railway strike and the
workers again attempted to make the strike general and to
win over the police. The strikers showed an extraordinary
militancy. They removed the rails in front of the manager's
train. They attacked it with sticks. They removed or
loosened the rails on curves or steep banks and at the approach to a bridge, pulled down telegraph poles and cut
wires to prevent telegraphic communication with the protectorate. In the words of the Governor, 'it was a revolt
against the state by its servants.' The municipality supported
the strike and the native press hinted at rebellion, whereupon the Governor suppressed the municipality. We have
here a very sharp division between the African labourers and
the employers in industry, mostly white.

In Gambia, a colony which is usually grouped with
Sierra Leone, the seamen are organized and in 1929 a sailors'
strike lasted 40 days and then grew into a general strike. At
the same time, the farmers, hostile over the low prices paid
for their products, carried on strenuous agitation. The people
were fired upon and nearly 50 were wounded. After three
weeks of the general strike, the Colonial Secretary addressed
a letter to the Union seeking arbitration. The Government
finally combined with the employers to defeat the strike.
This was not a revolt, but shows the capacity for organized
action which has developed in these older colonies, while an
outbreak which took place in Sierra Leone in February 1931,

shows the possibility of revolts infinitely more dangerous than any that have hitherto taken place. Hundreds of Negroes from the protectorate, led by an armed battalion of 50 men, invaded the Kambia district. The leader was Hahilara, a Negro Moslem leader who had converted thousands of natives to Mohammedanism, with which he united anti-imperialism. Hahilara called upon the peasants to refuse to pay taxes and to drive away the British officials. He demanded that all Crown lands in the protectorate should be confiscated and divided among the landless peasants. This was social revolution. Hahilara's agitation had widespread support. The Government attempted to arrest him, but the Negroes threatened to kill all Europeans who entered their territory. Government soldiers invaded the territory, and Hahilara was defeated and killed. But Captain H. J. Holmes, the officer commanding the British troops, was also killed. Hundreds of native huts were burnt to the ground and the rising was suppressed.

Yet perhaps the most significant feature of the revolt was the attitude of the Negro press in the colony, which emphasized the grievances of the insurgents in the protectorate. Sympathy among the intellectuals of Sierra Leone for the natives was widespread and the Sierra Leone workers were solid with the tribesmen. Should there be at any time a movement of the organized and educated blacks in the colony with a widespread peasant revolt in the protectorate, it would be difficult to prevent the Negroes of Sierra Leone and Gambia from gaining possession of the colony, though whether they would be able to keep it would depend upon events in other and wider spheres.

In Nigeria, a colony similar in social structure to Sierre Leone and Gambia, the crisis which began in 1929 produced the extraordinary women's revolt in which over 50 women were killed and over 50 wounded. The fall of prices for agrarian commodities placed the finances of the colony in difficulties, and the Government attempted to recuperate its falling revenues by an increase in direct taxation. Indirect rule works for the most part through chiefs, many of whom are merely instruments of the British Government. The chiefs were instructed to impose a tax upon the women whereupon the slumbering discontent broke out. Thousands of women organized protest demonstrations against the Government and its chiefs and at Aba, the capital of the Eastern Province, the women who sold in the market, faced with the possibility of a tax which would destroy their small profits, organized a revolt. The writer is informed by Africans from Nigeria that the actual happenings in Aba have been suppressed in all official reports. The women seized public buildings and held them for days. The servants refused to cook for their white masters and mistresses and some of them made the attempt to bring the European women by force into the markets to give them some experience of what work was like. These saved themselves only by precipitate flight, some of them with only the clothes they had on their backs. A detachment of soldiers suppressed the revolt, shooting at the black women as they tried to escape across the river. Martial law was proclaimed and the Governor called a meeting of the African editors in Lagos and threatened them with imprisonment if they published news of what was happening at Aba. That is why written evidence is confined to the official reports. A local committee of investigation was appointed and issued a report which was approved by the Legislative Council. Mr. Drummond Shiels, the Labour Under-Secretary of State for the Colonies, in answer to a question in the House of Commons replied that 'the Colonial Office was satisfied that the officials on the spot acted in the best interest of the country.' But the publication of the report was the signal for a widespread agitation throughout the colony. Mass meetings denounced it. The workers threatened to refuse to pay taxes; demanded a new commission, and redress of their economic and political grievances. The Government was forced to appoint another commission. The Negroes threatened to boycott it unless Africans were appointed and the Government was forced to appoint two. This commission admitted economic grievances and suggested measures of reform. The Governor, however, imposed a fine of £850 on the town of Aba. Such was the resentment aroused that the political officers appealed to the Governor to withdraw the fine, and again the Governor had to capitulate.

The strength and vigour of the movement were a shock to the Europeans. Sir Frank Baddeley, the Colonial Secretary of Nigeria, found that the revolt was the work of the agents of Moscow. *The Times* Correspondent, however, gave a more sober estimate.

'The trouble was of a nature and extent unprecedented in Nigeria. In a country where the women throughout the centuries have remained in subjection to the men, this was eventually a women's movement, organized, developed and carried out by the women, without either the help or commission of their menfolk, though probably with their tacit sympathy.'

Religious Revolts in New Colonies

The risings in Sierra Leone and Gambia are of a dual type. While the Negroes in the protectorates when driven to action think in terms of social revolution, those in the towns, like the majority of workers in Europe or America, aim at redress of immediate grievances, violent though their methods may be. Trade unions, the municipalities, the African press, have all given the movement its organized force, but of necessity make it more conservative.

In Eastern and Central Africa, more primitive territories, we have had during the last thirty years a series of risings of an entirely different type. In the years before the war, the tribes simply threw themselves at the government troops and suffered the inevitable defeat. Such risings could not go on. They were too obviously suicidal. In 1915, however, we have a new type—a rising led not by a tribal chief but by a Negro who has had some education. Such education as the African is given is nearly always religious, so that the leader often translated the insurrection into religious terms.

The Chilembwe rising in Nyasaland in 1915 was of this character. The first Europeans to arrive in Nyasaland were missionaries sent out by the Church of Scotland. Soon after, many of them left the mission for the land which they had acquired from the native chiefs. They set up as coffee planters, converting the natives jointly to Christianity and to cheap labour. By 1915, these plantations had passed into the hands of syndicates whose sole object was to make the maximum profit. Within these plantations which covered an area of 300 square miles and employed tens of thousands of Negroes, the companies permitted no school, no hospital and no missions.

A Negro, John Chilembwe by name, was sent to America by a small mission nearby. After having had a good education, he returned to his native land. He could find no position in any mission, so he built a church of his own with money raised from his fellow blacks. Most of the white men in Africa hate Africans who are educated and wear European clothes. His own treatment at the hands of the white planters and missionaries and his readings of the Bible, especially the story of the national struggle of the Jews in the Old Testament, inspired Chilembwe to lead a revolt against the European oppressors ('the Philistines').

Support for the revolt came mainly from the workers on the estate and, according to plan, the five European heads of the estate were killed. Their wives and children, however, met with great kindness. The blacks spent money to get eggs and milk for the white children, and banana leaves were held over their heads to protect them from the sun on their journey away from the estate.

The Europeans, frightened for their lives, ran to the military camps. But Chilembwe did not go very far. Just after he had preached a sermon in the church, with the estate manager's head on the pulpit, white police and soldiers appeared. The rebels took to the jungle, but were rigorously hunted down. Among those captured alive, about 20 were hanged, and all the rest sentenced to life terms. Chilembwe himself, old and nearly blind, was shot down in the long grass with the other leaders.

Six years after, in 1921, the greatest of the religious type of revolt occurred in the Belgian Congo, and shook the whole colony. The leader was Simon Kimbangu, a carpenter and a convert to Christianity. In the spring of 1921 he had a dream in which he was directed to go out and heal the sick. Kimbangu's influence immediately became very great among the native Christian converts. He appealed to the natives to leave the mission churches, controlled by their European masters, and to set up their own independent church organization under his guidance. To every African such a movement is an instinctive step towards independence and away from the perpetual control of Europeans. Negroes flocked in large numbers to Kimbangu, chiefly from the Protestant but from some of the Catholic missions as well. They declared they were tired of paying money to European churches.

The Government at first watched the movement uneasily but with tolerance. But the prophet's policy was soon seen to be detrimental to European interests in its implications. The natives left the plantations to listen to the Prophet, in much the same way as the Negro slaves in the West Indies a century before had been wont to plead religion and religious meetings as a convenient excuse for leaving the plantations at all times and without permission. The Negroes followed Kimbangu in such large numbers that industry was disorganized. Key plantations, upon which Government depended for the food for native employees in public utilities, were deserted. There was apprehension lest the natives should attempt to seize the lower Congo railway, which was indispensable to the colony. The fixing of Wednesday instead of Sunday as the day of rest created further dislocation. Worse still, as in all religious movements, minor 'prophets' sprang up in the wake of the master, all professing to work miracles, but all more extreme than the Prophet himself. Their preachings tended to become more and more anti-European. Wealthy natives in Kinshasa gave the movement financial and ideological support. Native students from the British and French colonies joined the movement and spread radical doctrines among the rank and file. The movement became so threatening that in June 1921 the Belgian Government ordered Kimbangu's arrest.

Like a true prophet, Kimbangu escaped and this served only to strengthen his hold upon the masses. He stayed in one village and was visited by thousands of his followers, yet remained free until September, a striking testimony to his own influence and the strength and solidarity of his organization.

He was eventually tried by court-martial in October. It was held that Kimbangu's organization had aimed at overthrowing the Belgian regime, and that religion was only a means of inciting the population. Kimbangu was sentenced to death, his lieutenants to sentences of imprisonment varying from one year to life-time, while a girl, Mandobe, described as the most revolutionary woman in the Congo, received two years. The Negroes reacted with great violence. Strikes immediately broke out everywhere, to such an extent that European traders at Thysville petitioned the King that Kimbangu should be publicly hanged. The Africans threatened that Kimbangu's death would be followed by a general massacre of the whites and the Home Government commuted Kimbangu's sentence to life imprisonment and deported many of the minor leaders. The movement has been crushed but the natives continue to expect the reappearance of their 'Messiah' and with it the departure of Europeans from the country.

We can conveniently deal here with the revolt of Africans in Kenya under the leadership of Harry Thuku. Harry Thuku, officially described as a man of base character, was very young, in his early twenties. He was a sort of petty clerk, and therefore had a little education, but he did not agitate in the name of God. He protested against high taxation, forced labour and other grievances. His propaganda touched even the smallest village and the state of an African colony is usually such that any strong leadership wins immediate support. The Thuku movement spread with great rapidity. It was estimated that at one meeting in Nairobi over 20,000 workers were enrolled.

Such a movement was too dangerous to be tolerated, and the Governor ordered mobilization of the native regiment, the King's African Rifles, to suppress it.

The Government supplemented force with trickery. It persuaded the chiefs to sign a proclamation appealing to the masses to return to work, and pledging the Government to reduce taxation and raise wages. This drove a wedge into

Thuku's organization. The more timid accepted these promises, the movement subsided and Thuku was arrested. The arrest at once brought the masses out again, ready for a general strike. Crowds swarmed round Thuku's prison demanding his release. The soldiers were ordered to fire upon the crowd, and more than 150 were killed. The Negroes, however, were not intimated. The Government circulated a rumour that Thuku would be transferred to another prison. This put the crowd on the wrong trail while Thuku was removed to a more remote and safer place. Hundreds were arrested, heavy fines were imposed, which in view of the low wages of the colony could only be liquidated by months of unremitting and unremunerative toil. All associations were declared illegal, and Thuku himself was shipped to Kismay on the Somali border, without trial.

The Congo

The Kimbangu movement took place in 1921. The Belgians, however, feared that there would be repetitions of the Kimbangu movement in a more extreme form. They were not mistaken. Indeed conditions in the Congo seem to produce an especially bitter and conscious type of revolt without any religious trimmings.

The difficulty here is to get accounts written in any detail. The British send out their punitive expeditions against revolting tribes and do not necessarily mention them in the annual colonial reports. But if the revolt awakens public interest, a commission will investigate and make a report. This report will frequently clash violently with the accounts of participants, eye-witnesses, correspondents of newspapers, native and European, and persons living in the colony at the time. The French and Belgians, however, publish little of this kind, and it is only indirectly that one can gain official confirmation of the vast revolts which have shaken the Belgian Congo since the days of Kimbangu. Thus, in the summer of 1932, M. Vandervelde, at one time Prime Minister of Belgium, spoke of the outrages in Belgian colonial administration and the revolts of the natives. In the course of his speech he said that lest he might make a mistake he had departed from his usual custom and was reading a part of his speech from notes. He told in detail the course of one revolt.

Three agents, sent to recruit workers in a Negro village, found only the women. The men, warned of their coming, had fled. The agents made the women kill cattle to feed them, then raped some of them. Some days after one of the Negroes, as is the custom in the Congo, demanded compensation. He was refused and lost his temper. He threw himself upon the white and bit him in the breast. This savage behaviour gained him a severe flogging from his masters, who had him whipped until he bled, then handed in an indictment against him. An investigation began, but the natives fell on the official and cut him to pieces. Followed the inevitable punitive expedition to restore law and order and the damaged prestige of the whites. The officer in command found that the natives had fled into the bush. To continue with the expedition meant that they would remain there and many children would starve to death. The Governor was adamant. 'We must', he telegraphed, 'carry out an act of authority and defend the prestige of the Government before the population.' The instruction was carried out. The natives fought back. They had only lances and other primitive weapons, but they fought for weeks. They died, says M. Vandervelde, in hundreds. But Lukutate, a native worker from Elizabethville, writing in the *Negro Worker* of July 1932, states that they died in thousands. Whole tribes, not knowing the effects of modern weapons, attacked the soldiers almost empty-handed. They starved in the forests. Some died under the whip, others were shot without trial in front of the women and children so as to warn them that blacks must never make rebellion against their white masters.

M. Vandervelde's account tallies very closely with that written by the Congo native. The files of the *Negro Worker* give many accounts of these revolts, and *The Life and Struggles of Negro Toilers*, by George Padmore, contains a great deal of co-ordinated information which is not easily obtainable elsewhere.

In 1924 there was a revolt in French Congo, lasting several days and suppressed by the French military authorities. In 1928, however, another revolt broke out, more class-conscious and better organized than the last. This lasted four months. The natives, despite the fewness of their arms, inflicted a number of defeats on the French troops, capturing a large section of the infantry. The fighting capacity of the revolutionaries, despite their handicaps, amazed even their enemies. The French shot all suspects, and whipped old men and women publicly in the villages as a warning. But by April 1930 the natives were rebelling again. A white French revolutionist and several natives were arrested at Brazzaville, capital of the Middle Congo, and sentenced to three years' imprisonment for attempting to organize a trade union. The natives, hearing of the sentence, went on strike and demonstrated before the court. The police attempted to break up the demonstration, but were attacked with stones. The soldiers were called out and without warning opened fire. The unequal fight continued until the natives were inevitably defeated. But the natives wounded the Governor of the Middle Congo, the troops had to occupy the native quarters of Brazzaville, and for days all business in the town was at a standstill.

This movement had definite Communist tendencies. What the authorities fear most is a combination of the workers in the towns and the peasants in the interior. Such a movement, however, has not yet taken place. The size of the territory, the differences of language, make such organization a task of great difficulty. Yet railways are linking the different portions of the territory, and in both French and Belgian Congo, French is becoming a *lingua franca* among those natives who get the chance to learn a little. Between 1921 and 1931 the whole temper of revolt in these territories has risen steadily. Since the war each succeeding revolt has been more fierce, more concentrated than the last.

Nor has the mandatory system made any essential difference. Ruanda-Urundi, formerly a part of German East Africa, is now mandated territory under the Belgian Government. Land alienation, or more precisely, taking away the natives' land, forced labour in the Katanga copper mines, all these typical features resulted in such a dislocation of local production, that the fields were not tilled and in 1929 a famine broke out in the district of Ruanda. Under the whip of hunger, the natives rose in revolt and the movement spread from Belgian Ruanda to British Uganda, where the tribes on the frontier also took up arms. The daughter of the King of Ruanda was one of the leaders of the revolutionaries, who made their first stroke at Gatsolon. There they killed a group of Belgian soldiers, officials, and native chiefs who were friendly with these whites. Belgian troops armed with modern weapons were brought to the scene, and against them the natives, armed only with spears and knives, battled for weeks. The masses of natives fled from the double scourge of famine and machine-guns. Where they fell, some of the bodies, still living, were devoured by wild animals. As was inevitable, the revolt was beaten down. The leaders fled through the swamps until they reached the Uganda frontier. There the British arrested them and handed them over to the Belgians. Over 1,000 tribesmen were shot and a Belgian regiment and a British detachment of the East African Rifles were stationed in Kiforte, the centre of the revolt.

The difference between the native under Belgian imperialism plain and simple, and Belgian imperialism carrying out the mandate of the League of Nations, is that the Belgian Government presents a report at Geneva on the working of the mandate. The native, however, is not likely to know this.

The Union of South Africa

The post-war period in South Africa has given us at least two clearly-marked types of Negro revolutionary activity, the Bondelzwarts revolt and the Industrial and Commercial Workers' Union. The Bondelzwarts revolt belongs in spirit to the early tribal revolts, that of the tribes beating their heads against a wall.

The Bondelzwarts are a tribe of Hottentots inhabiting the extreme southern portion of South-West Africa. They have actually never been fully conquered by Europeans, and their history is full of struggles against the Germans. After their last rebellion against the German Government, the leaders of the tribe, Jacobus Christian and Abraham Morris, were compelled to leave the territory and reside in the Cape Province. When the Germans were defeated during the war, Jacobus Christian asked the new authorities for permission to enter. He was refused. But in 1919, disregarding the Government's order, he returned to his native country. In April 1922, Abraham Morris, the other exiled leader, also returned home with a group of followers. On entering the territory he handed over his gun to the police, as required by the law. But the magistrate was not satisfied with that, and considering him a dangerous character, sent the police to arrest him and five of his followers. Morris resisted the arrest, and the people threatened to use violence on his behalf. When called upon to assist the police, all headmen refused, and the people working on the neighbouring farms abandoned their work and began to assemble at Haib, the headquarters of Jacobus Christian.

On May 12, Major van Coller with a police force was sent to effect the arrest of the 'five criminals'. He sent a message to Jacobus Christian to come and see him at Dreihoek, but, seeing the trap, Christian refused. The discontent of the people suddenly crystallized around their leader's arrest. Patrols of armed Hottentots forcibly collected arms from isolated European farmers, and at one farm, as the Administration later stated, 'European women were forced to prepare and pour out coffee for the Hottentots'.

On May 16, Jacobus Christian sent a statement to the Administrator stating that the five men would immediately report to the magistrate on condition that he received an assurance, in writing, from the Administrator, that no further steps would be taken against his people. This the Administrator refused to do, and both sides prepared for an armed struggle. Haib, the headquarters of the Bondelzwarts, was placed under martial law by Jacobus Christian. Armed pickets guarded all the roads and passers-by were subjected to the scrutiny of these guards. When Major van Coller, being unable to make Christian come to Dreihoek, was compelled to go to see him at Haib, he, a Major of the South-West African police, was stopped by armed pickets who allowed him to go to see the leader only after close examination. In his report he afterwards stated that the Bondelzwarts were all assembled and 'judging from their dispositions they are prepared to meet an armed force. They gave attentive hearing and showed no hostility towards us, but there was visible demurrence when they were told that arms and ammunition were to be surrendered'.

The struggle broke out on May 26, 1922. The forces of the rebels were very poor. The tribe had only six hundred men capable of bearing arms, and these six hundred had only about one hundred rifles. Against this ill-armed force, the

South African Government sent 445 well armed men, equipped with artillery, machine-guns, mechanical transport, and two aeroplanes. Yet the fighting lasted for nearly two weeks. The Bondelzwarts at first evaded big battles and tried to elude the Government forces. But they were surrounded and one big battle was fought in the mountains. Only the use of aeroplanes, something new and unexpected to the black warriors, compelled them to surrender. The number of killed will probably never be known. This was essentially a tribal revolt of the old pre-war type. But the resistance reached a pitch of calm determination to fight and die rather than give in, which makes it one of the most significant of African risings.

The Bondelzwarts revolt was an anachronism in 1922. The Union of South Africa is marked by a new type of political action—not the instinctive revolt of primitive tribes, but the militant action of the proletariat in the towns. Far more than in Sierra Leone and Gambia, South African industry has brought the natives together in factories, mines and on the docks, and the circumstances of their employment tended to drive them towards industrial organization in the modern manner. There is also the influence of the Russian Revolution. The South African Communist Party was founded only in 1924, but it had its origin in a previous organization which was already in existence in 1920. It directed its propaganda chiefly to the natives. But whereas in

Sierra Leone and Gambia the Negro intelligentsia of the Left for the moment are more vocal than effective, the South African system allows very few of these to exist and drives even the few that are there into militant opposition. From these post-war conditions and the economic and political crisis of 1919 sprang the Industrial and Commercial Workers' Union of South Africa.

It was formed in 1919 by a Nyasaland native, Clements Kadalie, and the organization began with only 24 members. Without any help in finance, experience or encouragement, suffering persecution and arrest, these built a movement which matured in strikes, demonstrations and battles with the police, while white South Africa watched its incredible growth with alarm. Kadalie, as a native of Nyasaland, could easily have been deported, but somehow he escaped this fate and drove his movement forward.

The first sign of the I.C.U.'s real strength was the Port Elizabeth strike of 1920. The Port Elizabeth workers, mainly unskilled labourers, had demanded and obtained an increase of sixpence a day. In February 1920, a branch of the I.C.U. was formed in Port Elizabeth. This demanded a further increase of sixpence a day and as a consequence of fresh agitation, the workers obtained it. But this did not satisfy them and, on the advice of Kadalie, the President of the I.C.U., they advanced a demand for a minimum daily wage of ten shillings for unskilled male workers and seven shillings and sixpence for adult females. Meetings were held all over the district by the I.C.U., at which workers were called upon to insist on this demand even to the point of a strike. This I.C.U. agitation had a tremendous effect. Feeling was running high and the influence of Kadalie was increasing. At one meeting, the feelings of the workers were so aroused that some made a physical attack on Dr. Rubusama, also a Negro, who was known to be opposed to Kadalie. Dr. Rubusama was only rescued by Kadalie who, on seeing his danger, immediately intervened.

The police, in the meanwhile, were looking for an excuse to arrest Kadalie. This attack on Dr. Rubusama was used as a pretext. Rubusama made an affidavit concerning the attack on him, and Kadalie was arrested on October 23, 1920, without a warrant.

When news of the arrest became known, the workers congregated in the nearest square. A meeting was held and a deputation was sent to the police to ask for the release of Kadalie on bail. The chief of police refused. When the deputation returned with this news the meeting resolved to send an ultimatum to the police: unless Kadalie was released by five o'clock, they would release him themselves. The South African native was openly challenging not only white employers but the actual forces of the state.

The whole police force was armed. The railway police were called out. In addition, European volunteers were

armed and stationed in front of the police station where
Kadalie was detained. By five o'clock the demonstration
numbered 3,000 people.

The mounted police were ordered to charge, but they
were unhorsed. An attempt was made to disperse the crowd
by means of a water-hose. But the masses replied with stones
and other missiles. At this stage two shots were fired and the
crowd began to retreat. It was at this moment, while the
crowd was running, that the police opened fire upon it. The
official Commission of Inquiry stated: '. . . it is established
beyond doubt that immediately after the first shots were
fired, the crowd stampeded in all directions, and that a rapid
and sustained fusillade was directed on the retreating crowd
from the police station for 60 seconds, as alleged by some
witnesses, or two minutes as alleged by others. One civilian
admitted firing 15 shots; another as many as 13 shots, with
the most fatal results, viz.: 1 European and 23 natives or
coloured males were killed or died of wounds. Native and
coloured males wounded, 45; females, 1. European females
wounded, 4. Total casualties, 76. Only two of these were
shot immediately in front of the steps, the others fell in different parts of the street away from the police station, as far
as Castle Street, 100 yards distant.' Obviously the police
were seizing the opportunity to smash the workers' organization once and for all. The net result, as so often, was to increase its strength.

So powerful a force did the I.C.U. become among the Bantu and coloured people that Hertzog, a future Prime Minister of South Africa, thought it profitable to seek the support of the I.C.U. in the Cape Province. He sent a very cordial letter to Kadalie, enclosing a donation to the I.C.U., saying that he was sorry that he could not do more.

Of course, immediately Hertzog gained power, he persecuted the I.C.U. even more fiercely. But the movement continued to grow, and in 1926 it reached its peak. In that year it had a membership of 100,000. Teachers were leaving the profession to become agents of the I.C.U. In remote villages of South Africa one could find a representative. Many who had not joined rallied to it in time of difficulty.

It will be difficult to over-estimate what Kadalie and his partner, Champion, achieved between 1919 and 1926. Kadalie was an orator, tall, with a splendid voice, and at his meetings he used to arouse the Bantu workers to great heights of enthusiasm. At the conclusion of the speech his hearers were usually silent for some seconds before they were able to begin the applause. Champion was the very opposite of Kadalie in everything. More backward in outlook than Kadalie, who was aware of the working-class movement as an international force, he saw very little beyond Zululand, or Natal, and he was more organizer than orator.

The real parallel to this movement is the mass uprising in San Domingo. There is the same instinctive capacity for organization, the same throwing-up of gifted leaders from among the masses. But whereas there was a French Revolution in 1794 rooting out the old order in France, needing the black revolution, and sending out encouragement, organizers and arms, there was nothing like that in Britain. Seen in that historical perspective, the Kadalie movement can be understood for the profoundly important thing it was.

After 1926 the movement began to decline. It could not maintain itself for long at that pitch without great and concrete successes. It was bound to stabilize itself at a less intense level. Kadalie lacked the education and the knowledge to organize it on a stable basis—the hardest of all tasks for a man of his origin. There was misappropriation of the funds. He saw the necessity for international affiliation. But though the constitution of the organization condemned capitalism, he would not affiliate to the Third International. The white South African workers refused his offer of unity, for these, petty-bourgeois in outlook owing to their high wages and the social degradation of the Negro, are among the bitterest enemies of the native workers. Kadalie came to Europe, affiliated the I.C.U. to the International Federation of Trade Unions and sought the help of left-wing Labour members. He took back a white man, Ballinger, to assist him. But the decline of the I.C.U. continued. The organization split. To-day the two sections are but a shadow of the early I.C.U., and Kadalie keeps a café in Port Elizabeth, where formerly the workers had been shot down while demonstrating for his release.

Chapter 5

Marcus Garvey

During the very period, 1919–1926, that the natives in South Africa were organizing themselves, a similar movement was taking place among the Negroes in America. A large population, more literacy, the greater wealth of the Negro and greater facilities for publicity and communication, made this movement the biggest Negro organization yet known. It is known as the Garvey Movement.

To understand the Garvey Movement one must have some idea of the status of the Negro even in modern America. The period of 'reconstruction' did not last long and the Southern whites soon re-established their old domination on the new basis of Negro freedom. In many areas they prevented the Negro from voting, either by inventing fantastic qualifications such as those which find a Negro graduate of Harvard or Yale unable to exercise the franchise through lack of education; or quite simply by parading armed men before the polling booth and warning the Negro what would happen to him if he attempted to come near. In states such as Texas, the Negro is made to feel his colour at every turn. He cannot ride in the Pullman cars, he must sit at the back of the street-cars; in certain areas he can own only a Ford car; the white always has the right of way in the street. The Negro must make up his mind that his black skin makes him a servant and he must remain so. Periodically, some years at the rate of more than one a week, a Negro is lynched by a howling mob of white citizens. In the more liberal North there is race prejudice though it is not nearly so acute.

Both in North and South, certain Negroes have emerged as business men, professional men, artists, writers, musicians. Some of them do astonishingly well and the circle of Negro intelligentsia is daily increasing. Yet the prevailing attitude to the Negro is one of strong and sometimes ferocious prejudice.

Before the Negro can struggle intelligently against this, in order that the layman may appreciate the efforts which have been made and the possibilities of success, it is necessary to inquire more closely as to the origin of this powerful prejudice which inevitably awakens kindred feelings in the Negroes. There is no question here as in Africa of alien civilizations. The American Negro, in language, tradition and culture is an American. He was in America almost from the beginning and he has helped to make the country what it is. Hostility to him on the part of the whites is not a question of physiological repugnance. The numerous half-breeds, the unceasing miscegenation in America as well as in so strong a fortress of race prejudice as South Africa, prove this. That the colour bar exists only in day-light is a proverb common in Africa as well as in America. A Southern white woman will be nursed by a Negro wet-nurse, and will pass her childhood days with Negro servants. As she grows up she will be taught to ride by a black groom. Black servants will cook her food and wait on her at table. A young Southern woman, it is common knowledge, often has far more confidence in her old black nurse than in her own relations. A black chauffeur will drive her into town. She enters a restaurant, sees a Negro sitting 40 feet away having a meal, and shrieks that he must be put out. Obviously she feels no physical repugnance. This is a social and political question. The Negro must be kept in his place. This is the main reason for the Southern persecution of the Negro. As worker, as tenant-farmer, as sharecropper, he is at the mercy of his employer and he must be terrorized into acceptance of whatever conditions of life are offered to him. What are the reasons usually offered for the attitude of the Southern whites towards Negroes? Sex is the one most usually urged: the Negro cannot subdue his passion for white women. Yet of 130 Negro revolts that took place between 1670 and 1865 in America, there is not a single case recorded of a white woman being raped by the revolting slaves. In the West Indies, since the abolition of slavery, there has not been one single case of rape or sexual assault by a Negro against a white woman. While the thousands of cases of Negroes lynched in America during the last half-century, charges of rape have been made in only twenty per cent. of cases. With what justification some of these charges have been made the Scottsboro' case has within recent years given a glaring example. It is not strange that this is so. Sir Harry Johnston after his vast experience of Africa shows on what ground similar agitation has been raised against African Negroes.

> There is, I am convinced, a deliberate tendency in the Southern States to exaggerate the desire of the Negro for a sexual union with white women and the crimes he may commit under this impulse. A few exceptional Negroes in West and South Africa, and in America, are attracted towards a white consort, but almost invariably for honest and pure-minded reasons, because of some intellectual affinity or sympathy. The mass of the race, if left free to choose, would prefer to mate with women of its own type. When cases have occurred in the history of South Africa, South-West, East and Central Africa, of some great Negro uprising, and the wives and daughters of officials, missionaries and settlers have been temporarily at the mercy of a Negro army, or in the power of a Negro chief, how extremely rare are the proved cases of any sexual abuse arising from this circumstance! How infinitely rarer than the prostitution of Negro women following on some great conquest of their whites or of their black or yellow allies! I know that the contrary has been freely alleged and falsely stated in histories of African events; but when the facts have been really investigated, it is little else than astonishing that the Negro has either had too great a racial sense of decency, or too little liking for the white women (I believe it to be the former rather than the latter) to outrage

the unhappy white women and girls temporarily in his power. He may have dashed out the brains of the white babies against a stone, have even killed, possibly, their mothers, or taken them and the unmarried girls as hostages into the harem of a chief (where no attempt has ever been made upon their virtue), but in the history of the various Kaffir wars it is remarkable how in the majority of cases the wives and daughters of the British, the Boers, and the Germans, after the slaughter of their male relations, were sent back unharmed to white territory.

All Negroes are aware of the mass of lies on which the prejudice is built, of the propaganda which is designed to cover the naked economic exploitation. But the Negro and his white friends have little chance to stem the propaganda. The main organs of publicity are in the hands of the whites. The millions who watch the films always see Negroes shining shoes or doing menial work, singing or dancing. Of the thousands of Negro professional men, of the nearly two hundred Negro universities and colleges in America which give degrees in every branch of learning, and are run predominantly by Negro professors, of this the American capitalist takes good care that nothing appears on the screen.

Thus the American Negro, literate, Westernized, an American almost from the foundation of America, suffers from his humiliations and discriminations to a degree that few whites and even many non-American Negroes can ever understand. The jazz gaiety of the American Negro are a semi-conscious reaction to the fundamental sorrow of the race. Often lynching is not the spontaneous madness of a crowd, but a demonstration carefully organized and announced in the press as being fixed for the next day. The American whites will burn a Negro alive. Less than ten years ago a crowd of white men, women and children danced round a burning Negro singing 'Happy days are here again.' Little by little the Negro in the South, particularly in the towns, is fighting his way to better conditions. But the continuity of white policy is unbroken from 1650 to 1930. The Negro must be kept down. That is the background of Negro American life.

During the war thousands of Negroes emigrated from the South to the North where there was work to be had, high pay, and racial discrimination was less offensive. Negro soldiers fought in the war and suffered not only from the race prejudice of their own officers, but, welcomed by the French, saw the American whites, by word and deed and written memoranda, seek to poison the French against them. So fiercely did the white Americans attack them that the French asked to take them over. The black regiment was brigaded with a French division and fought as a French unit. The first American to win the *Croix-de-Guerre* was a Negro. The regiment fought with great gallantry and when the war was over the French General Staff, appreciative and courteous according to their lights, gave these visitors the honour of being the first allied regiment to march into German territory. This did not make the blacks love the Americans any better. They came home bitter and disillusioned, to find that they had shed their blood in the war for democracy and faced the same undemocratic conditions as before.

In August 1914, Marcus Garvey, a Jamaican Negro, a printer, and Amy Ashwood, his friend, almost a school-girl, founded the Universal Negro Improvement Association in Kingston, Jamaica. They were the only members, and she appointed him the President, and he appointed her the Secretary. They carried on propaganda in Jamaica for two years, and then Garvey went to the United States, the Mecca of all West Indian Negroes before the slump. Amy Ashwood went to New York to meet him in 1918, and the U.N.I.A. then had 17 members. Garvey spoke and agitated, and by 1919 he had about 5,000 members attached to his organization. Then he got arrested for libelling the Assistant District Attorney of New York. Negroes all over America were suddenly aware of him. The soldiers were coming back home, bringing their bitterness and their money. There was a boom and Negroes shared in it. Revolution was in the air, and the Negroes were ready for revolution.

There has never been a Negro movement anywhere like the Garvey Movement, and few movements in any country can be compared to it in growth and intensity. By 1920 it was proportionately the most powerful mass movement in

America. Supporters of Garvey have claimed that the U.N.I.A. membership in 1920 reached three millions, and Garvey himself claimed in 1924 six millions. The latter figure is certainly exaggerated, for that would have meant at least half of the total Negro population of America at that time. That nine-tenths of the Negroes in America were listening to him is probable, and as far as can be gathered, from very insufficient data, he may well have had two million members already in 1920. Money and members poured in from every state in America, from all over the West Indies, from Panama. Negroes sold their dearest possessions to send money to Garvey. His name rolled through Africa. The King of Swaziland told a friend some years after that he knew the names of only two black men in the Western world, Jack Johnson and Marcus Garvey.

What was Garvey's programme? Back to Africa. The Negroes must have Africa back for themselves. They would go and settle there and live in Africa as free and happy as Europeans lived in Europe and white Americans in America. How were they to get Africa back? They would ask the imperialists for it, and if the imperialists did not give it, they would take it back. That was in essence all that Garvey had to say. True, he attacked lynching, he formulated militant demands, equal rights for Negroes, democratic liberties, etc. But the programme was essentially, Back to Africa.

It was pitiable rubbish, but the Negroes wanted a lead

and they took the first that was offered them. Furthermore, desperate men often hear, not the actual words of an orator but their own thoughts. Daniel O'Connell preached the Repeal of the Union, but the large majority of Irish peasants thought in terms of the expulsion of the British and the seizure of the land. And Garvey was a man of exceptional gifts. He was an orator, at his best a very great orator indeed, opportunist to the bone, skilful in tuning his words to his audience. But his words were always militant, and the Negroes listened, paid their money and waited. All the things that Hitler was to do so well later Garvey was doing in 1920 and 1921. He organized storm-troopers, who marched, uniformed, in his parades, and kept order and gave colour to his meetings. He understood what was then supposed to be the psychology of the Negro with his child-like mentality. (But this was before some of the greatest peoples in Europe were swept off their feet by the same antics and promiscuous promises.) And while Garvey whipped up his audiences, like Hitler, he organized his millions of adherents with a German thoroughness.

It is not improbable that the strength of the movement he had unloosed took Garvey by surprise. He and his wife covered the country, enrolling members. He built a hall, Liberty Hall, he organized mass demonstrations and congresses. He appointed himself President, Emperor, King and what not, of Africa, and created a string of Negro nobility,

and titled followers, from Dukes to plain baronets. He sent
deputations to the League of Nations asking for Africa. He
embarked on a steamship scheme, the Black Star Line, and
actually bought one or two ships which actually made one or
two voyages. 'The Black Star Line will sail to Africa if it sails
in seas of blood.' But programme for the Afro-Americans he
had none, not even a bad one.

Despite his militancy, furthermore, Garvey was confused. He attacked imperialism, but he was ready to
propound the doctrine that the Negro must be loyal to all
flags under which he lives. He viciously attacked Communism and advised the Negro workers against linking up
with white workers in industrial struggles. He negotiated with
the Ku Klux Klan for the repatriation of Negroes to Liberia.
From about 1921 it was already clear that his aims were beyond achievement. But he was a man of great physical
courage, he continued to hold great meetings, some of them
in Madison Square, with police constantly striving to arrest
him, and sometimes succeeding. He indulged in some un-
sound business schemes. He sent agents to Liberia, but the
Liberian Government, satellites of America, would have little
to do with them, and it is doubtful if Garvey ever intended
to do anything serious. Yet for years he continued to have
a huge mass following and exercised a powerful influence
on millions of Negroes in America and all over the world. In
1926 he was charged for using the United States mail with

intent to defraud. He was convicted, imprisoned, and then deported to Jamaica. There he at once began an evolution the signs of which had long been evident. He quickly made his peace with British imperialism. His movement disintegrated.

One thing Garvey did do. He made the American Negro conscious of his African origin and created for the first time a feeling of international solidarity among Africans and people of African descent. In so far as this is directed against oppression it is a progressive step. But his movement was in many respects absurd and in others thoroughly dishonest. It has resulted in a widespread disillusionment. Unlike Kadalie, he was petty-bourgeois in origin and never thought in terms of industrial organization. Yet the Garvey Movement like the I.C.U. in its best days, though it actually achieved little in proportion to its size, is of immense importance in the history of Negro revolts. It shows the fires that smoulder in the Negro world, in America as in Africa.

Chapter 6

Negro Movements in Recent Years

In the British Empire there have been a series of Negro movements since the Ottawa Conference in 1932. This drove cheap Japanese goods out of the colonies and brought in British just at the time when the blacks were impoverished by the world crisis. The ensuing response to subversive propaganda led to the passing of drastic sedition bills. Thus the colonies have been, in recent years, the scene of revolt after revolt, in the West Indies, in West Africa, in East Africa, and Mauritius. Let us take some of these revolts and try to analyse their particular significance.

The Gold Coast, one of the old colonies, has recently experienced an upheaval. In 1937, in the Gold Coast and in Ashanti, a district in the interior, the cocoa farmers organized themselves against the 'Pool' set up by the commercial firms and made up their minds to smash it. Early in 1938 the motor drivers, protesting against heavy fines for trivial offences (imposed by an African magistrate) struck, and brought motor traffic to a standstill. The boat-boys went on strike. The strike was general, and a boycott of European merchandise was proclaimed. Anyone found buying or selling European imported goods was assaulted, carried before a chief and penalized. Sir Ofori Atta, a typical Government chief, supported the strike, so strong was the pressure of the masses. The population of Cape Coast, a sea-port town in the Gold Coast, staged a mass demonstration against a new water-rate. The police tried to interfere and were driven back to the station, which was razed to the ground. The Government ordered police and soldiers to Cape Coast. Their way lay through Saltpond. The people of Saltpond barricaded the road and resisted the soldiers and police, who were driven back. By the time they reached Cape Coast all was calm.

An extraordinary determination and unity linked the population. An unconfirmed report stated that, being owners of their land, the Cape Coast people gave notice to the United Africa Company, Lord Leverhulme's combine, to quit, this by way of protest against the water-rate. At the expiration of the notice they forced the stores open and put the goods outside. Owing to the motor strike there were no lorries to take these away, and they were looted.

Militant as was this movement, yet, as in most of the older colonies, there was not that militancy which thinks in terms of throwing out the British. The West Africans are increasingly proud, nationalistic, jealous of discrimination, but there is no national revolutionary movement. A Cocoa Commission from Britain helped to restore quiet and is preparing a report.

In the West Indian colony of Trinidad there has been an even more powerful movement.

The victory of the San Domingo blacks gave the final blow to the slave-trade in the West Indies. Britain abolished the trade in 1807 and slavery itself was abolished in 1834, due to the economic decline of the West Indies, the vigorous attacks of the abolitionists, and the support of the new industrial bourgeoisie to whom the privileges of the West Indies sugar planters were detrimental. The great insurrection in Jamaica in 1831 contributed materially to hasten the process. The Negroes in the West Indian islands have therefore developed in a manner peculiar to themselves. The blacks speak French, English or Spanish. They have lost all sense of their African origin and have become Westernized in their outlook. A Negro and Mulatto middle-class has emerged. Racial prejudice and discrimination, though by no means abolished, have gradually declined. Though the whites control most of the industries, the Negro middle-classes are gradually monopolizing the professions and the civil service. The Negroes are not a minority as in America, are trained in the Western manner, and the whites therefore cannot take undue liberties with them.

Socially the situation is in no way comparable to that in Central or Southern Africa or the Southern States. In Trinidad a few years ago a white South African was appointed to a post in the civil service. For some reason or other he kicked a black labourer who immediately kicked him back. The South African was charged. The magistrate on the bench, a coloured man, fined him. He was made to understand that he was no longer in South Africa, and that if he did not mend his ways, he would be sent to prison. Most of the colonies are governed by the Colonial Office, and driven by the confused, but steady pressure of the masses for improvement, the Colonial Office evades the issue by appointing more and more men of colour to the higher posts in the service. The islands produce coloured men of great intellectual brilliance who have distinguished careers in the inns of court, the hospitals and in the British universities. The coloured middle-classes are making great progress. They grumble at racial discrimination, but their outlook is the same as that of the rich whites, and indeed their sole grievances are that they do not get all the posts they want, and that the whites do not often invite them to dinner.

The real difficulty of the West Indies is the poverty of the masses. The islands have been steadily declining in economic importance. The black and Mulatto intelligentsia sometimes use radical phases, but for the most part are interested solely in their own advancement. The Henry Norman Commission at the end of the last century recommended the break-up of the large estates and the spread of peasant proprietorship, but the officials and the nominated members of the Legislative Councils do not concern themselves with such projects, and malnutrition, bad housing conditions and low wages seemed to be the permanent fate of the Negro masses. The 1929 crisis and Ottawa have increased the burden on the poor. This situation has resulted in growing radicalization of the masses, a sharpening of racial feeling and a growing social and political tension in the islands. It reached its climax in Trinidad last year, and that the movement assumed the proportions that it did in Trinidad is no accident, and shows how human nature responds to environment, in London, China and Peru.

Trinidad has a population of some four hundred thousand people, of whom over one-third are Indians, the descendants of men and women brought to the island from India as indentured labourers. Between them and the blacks there is no racial ill-feeling. As in South Africa and America, 1919 was a period of great unrest in the West Indies. There was a general strike of the dockers. They patrolled the town, made business close down, and were at one time in charge of the city. The white industrialists clamoured that cruisers should be sent for and the mere landing of armed sailors was sufficient to restore the *status quo*. There was little organized industry, and as in Barbados, even up to the present day, artisans and unskilled labourers find it difficult to organize themselves. The writer was in the island at that time, and one feature of the disturbances caused widespread comment in informed circles: while the workers were in control of the

town, the police were singularly inactive. It was stated that
the officer in command was subjected to an inquiry and made
good his contention that he could not trust his black police-
men to shoot at the black workers. Race feeling is not acute
at normal times. Children of all colours are educated together at the secondary schools. Whites, blacks, browns,
Indians and Chinese, play cricket and football together on
afternoons, sometimes in the same team, and the various
members of the community turn out to cheer their respective
sides. West Indian cricket teams composed of all colours tour
England and Australia together without undue friction and
with a great deal of friendliness in many cases. But the division of rich and poor is also the division of white and black,
and in moments of tension can become very acute. For the
same reason, however, the possibility is greater here than
elsewhere, that the police might take sides with the workers,
and that is an ever present difficulty which is to be solved by
the cruiser—as long as cruisers are available.

Between 1919 and 1937 Trinidad, like the other West
Indian islands, has lived an increasingly active political life.
Self-government is one of the questions of the day, and the
Legislative Council now has elected members. What has
created the new Trinidad, however, has been the development of the oil industry, which now employs nearly 10,000
men concentrated in the southern part of the island. Large-
scale industry has had the inevitable result of developing a

high sense of labour solidarity and growing political consciousness. The slump threw the population into great poverty and the inadequacy of the social services intensified the resultant suffering. The Ethiopian question sharpened the sense of racial solidarity and racial oppression. News of the stay-in strikes in France and America was eagerly read by these workers. They found a leader in Uriah Butler, an agitator with a religious bias.

Butler's career, despite his religion, is identical with that of many revolutionaries in Western Europe. Since the war the leader of the workers' movement in Trinidad has been Captain Cipriani, a white man who identified himself with the interests of the black masses and did very fine work on their behalf. His Labour Party is a loose political organization, which protected the industrial interests of the workers as far as it could, agitated for self-government and was for years the only mass political organization in the island. But Cipriani is a reformist. Butler was a member of this party, he wanted militant industrial action and was expelled for holding 'Communistic' views and being 'extremist'. He went to the South and carried on his agitation among the oilfield workers. In June of last year the oilfield workers staged a stay-in strike for higher wages. The consequences were unprecedented.

The Government tried to arrest Butler while he was addressing a crowd. The crowd resisted the arrest and the police had to retire. One Corporal King, a Negro (notorious in the district for his hostility to the workers), followed Butler. He was set upon by the crowd, and in attempting to escape, fell and broke his leg. While he lay on the ground he was beaten, oil was poured upon him and he was burned to death. The episode is almost identical with the lynchings of Negroes in the Southern states. King was a black man, but his whole career had identified him with the whites, and reports from the island state that the regrets expressed are not for the burning but that it was not one of 'them'—meaning the whites. Later in the day the police were fired upon and a sub-inspector was killed.

Thenceforth the strike spread. Destruction of property may have been the work of certain hooligan elements, as the official report states, but the strike was complete in Port-of-Spain, the capital, a town of 80,000 inhabitants, which is at the opposite end of the island, some 40 miles away from the scene of the first outbreak. This, the most outstanding feature of the disturbances, is referred to parenthetically in the official report as follows: 'The same morning Port-of-Spain, where work at all the industrial establishments had ceased. . . .' The Indian agricultural labourers, who might appear to have little in common with the black proletariat, no sooner saw these blacks in militant action than they too followed them and began to strike. In many parts of the island stoppage of work was complete. The Government sent

for one cruiser. But whereas in 1919 the unrest subsided at
the appearance of the sailors, much has happened since then,
and the people were quite unmoved at the appearance of the
first, and even of a second, cruiser. The Governor had taken
a strong line at first, but, in the face of the determination of
the population, he and one of the leading officials used language hostile to the white employers and attempted concilia-
tion. The Governor has been censured for this and has now
retired from the colonial service. His action was probably
justified. Though the Commission's report denies it, information from the spot states that race feeling was rampant,
and it needed little to precipitate a general attack on the
whites. It could hardly have been otherwise, for the Governor himself stressed the importance of the Ethiopian question in sharpening the political tension in the island. The
majority of Negroes everywhere have the misguided belief
that the blacks of Ethiopia were betrayed by the whites because they were black. The Commission has admitted the
grievous condition of the poor in the island, and have thus
indirectly justified the strike. What is important, however,
is the political awakening which it has crystallized. The
Commission's report merely hints at, but does not state that,
the workers demanded the forty-hour week, holidays with
pay, and it is stated, though this is not as yet certain, a share
of the profits. They demanded equal pay with white men for
the same work, they showed their resentment against South

African whites who have attempted to treat them in a way to which they have not been accustomed. After returning to work they again went on strike to force recognition of their newly formed union. Captain Cipriani, their idol for years, was not in the island at the time of the strike and spoke against them. They threw him and his party over at once. Trade unions are being formed all over the island, and the advanced workers are clamouring for revolutionary literature of all sorts, by Marx and Engels and other writers on Communism, and literature dealing with the Ethiopian question. In the recent elections, in the key Southern constituency, the workers' candidate was Mr. Rienzi, an Indian lawyer, president of the new unions. Some of his opponents tried to raise the race question, Negro as opposed to Indian. But Rienzi had fought with them side by side all through the days of the strike. They refused to be distracted. They and their leaders poured scorn on the racial question and proclaimed that the issue was one of class. Thus these workers have almost at a single bound placed themselves in the forefront of the international working-class movement. The Government is now seeking to pass a drastic bill imposing heavy penalties for the mere possession of radical far less revolutionary literature. The white employers are calling for soldiers to be stationed in the island. It is certain that racial feeling will gradually take a less prominent part in the struggle than hitherto, for the Negro middle-classes are already aligning themselves and

making the issue clear. They are with the whites. Indus-
trialization has been the decisive factor here. While it is
unwise to predict, the clamour for literature shows how
strong is the urge to know what is happening abroad and
follow suit. Already a local pamphlet has been written on
Fascism. The movement is clearly on its way to a link with
the most advanced workers in Western Europe. This is a
stage far beyond the Gold Coast. This study was already in
proof when the Jamaica revolt forced the appointment of a
Royal Commission. The Negroes in British Guiana are also
simmering with unrest. In Trinidad mass demonstrations are
still taking place. The history of all these territories is in
essence the history of Trinidad. Consideration of the
remedies is beyond us but they will need to be far-reaching.

The third and last of the recent revolts selected for treatment here took place as far back as 1935. Yet it is of more
importance than the other two. Trinidad is but a small
island in the West Indies, the coastal districts of West Africa
are but a fringe to the millions of Negroes in Central, East
and Southern Africa. The report of the Commission of Inquiry on the revolt of the Rhodesian miners in 1935 gives a
very clear picture of what is going on in the mind of the great
masses of Africans.

Northern Rhodesia is a new type of colony. It is like
Kenya in that there is no sort of buffer class in between the
white settlers and the Negroes. There is, however, an indus-

trial proletariat in the copper mines, and this at once gives native resentment weight. The wages are round about fifteen shillings a month, with the usual complement of seg- regation and racial discrimination. In October 1935, there was a strike in the mines. The tax had been abruptly raised and the workers protested in the only way they could. Soldiers were rushed to the spot, six natives were killed and 22 wounded, and peace restored. From all appearances this is hardly a revolt, but merely a strike which has got out of hand. Such a view would completely misunderstand the present situation in Africa and be wholly false. This, for instance, is a native translation of the call for the strike.

> Listen to this all you who live in the country, think well how they treat us and to ask for a land. Do we live in good treatment, no; therefore let us ask one another and re- member this treatment. Because we wish on the day of 29th April, every person not to go to work, he who will go to work, and if we see him it will be a serious case. Know how they cause us to suffer, they cheat us for money, they arrest us for loafing, they persecute us and put us in gaol for tax. What reason have we done? Secondly do you not wish to hear these words, well listen, this year of 1935, if they will not increase us more money stop paying tax, do you think they can kill you, no. Let us encourage surely you will see that God will be with us. See how we suffer with the work and how we are continually reviled and beaten underground. Many brothers of us die for 22s. 6d., is this money that we should lose our lives for. He who

cannot read should tell his companion that on the 29th April not to go to work. These words do not come from here, they come from the wisers who are far away and enable to encourage us.

That all. Hear well if it is right let us do so.

We are all of the Nkana

Africans—Men and Women.

I am glad,

G. LOVEWEY.

It is clear that this is no mere appeal to strike but a summons to relentless struggle with mortal enemies. Should world events give these people a chance, they will destroy what has them by the throat as surely as the San Domingo blacks destroyed the French plantocracy. This note of having endured to the limit and being ready to resist to the death occurs in another notice found by accident which states: 'Nobody must go to work on the 1st May. All tribes and people. We shall die. They will kill us on Friday. P.W.' The summons to strike makes a reference to the 'wisers far away', i.e., probably those who are more intelligent than we and are guiding us. The official investigation shows that the Watch Tower Movement has some influence among the Rhodesian natives.

Watch Tower is a secret society originating in America. It issues political tracts and pamphlets. It has headquarters in Cape Town and its representatives hold meetings in Rhodesia and for that matter all over South Africa. The Watch

Tower bases its teaching on the second coming of Christ. Having on previous occasions foretold the exact date it does not do so any longer, but it confidently expects Christ and things that when he comes the government of the world will be delivered into his hands. This is not very different from the doctrine of the missionaries. But Watch Tower goes on to declare that all the governments which are ruling the world, especially Great Britain and the United States of America, are organizations of Satan, and that all churches, especially the Protestant and Roman Catholic churches, are emissaries of Satan. Religion thus becomes a weapon in the class struggle.

All the Watch Tower books and pamphlets preach a transparent doctrine. The Devil's organization is made up 'principally of those that rule and that are called the official part of the nation.' Governments are 'the Beast', particularly the seventh World Power, which is Great Britain. 'The League of Nations is against God and his anointed, but who is primarily responsible for the League of Nations compact?' The Devil is its father, the British Empire its mother. '. . . Catholicism is an abomination in the sight of the Lord, but the Protestants are even more abominable than Catholics.' Organized Christianity is full of filthiness, full of 'hypocrisy, abomination, fornication and filthiness. Under the present form of government the people suffer much injustice and are greatly oppressed. Their taxes are high, while the products of their labour are low in price. . . . The facts are that a great change from an extremely selfish government to one that is wholly unselfish and righteous is just at hand'.

The illustrations preach corresponding sentiments with a greater vigour. One feature for instance displays four people quarrelling over a prone body. One is a fat gross European in a dress suit with top hat and hunting crop. The second is a similar figure in a frock coat and with a bag of money. The third is a European apache with a drawn dagger in his hand. The fourth is a fat Bishop with a mitre. Behind is the devil spurring them on. This is supposed to represent Universal War.

It is difficult to say exactly the true influence of the Watch Tower. The writer has been informed by Negro sailors that its influence is widely spread throughout Africa, and that it is the most powerful revolutionary force in Africa to-day. The Gentle Jesus, meek and mild, of the missionaries cannot compete with the Watch Tower God. The Commission which inquired into Rhodesian 'disturbances' recognized its importance and devoted many pages to it.

Such are the ideas moving in the minds of these African copper miners. They are absurd only on the surface. They represent political realities and express political aspirations far more closely than programmes and policies of parties with millions of members, numerous journals and half a century of history behind them. Watch Tower says what the thinking native thinks and what he is prepared to die for.

In his *The Native Problem in Africa,* Dr. Buell makes one very noteworthy observation: 'The extreme credulity with which natives, under the spell of a leader claiming divine or mystical power, will throw away their material interests and recklessly sacrifice their lives is one of the most amazing features of Africa to-day. The African native is, however, not likely to express this type of fanaticism in a deliberate attack upon European authority. But he has already demonstrated an extraordinary power of passive resistance which will make the problem of control more difficult than if the native population attempted to massacre the Europeans in cold blood.'

This apparent fanaticism is the best indication to the true feeling of many millions of Africans. They know what they want, but they do not know what to do. Except in colonies like Sierra Leone and Gambia and to some degree among the Negro intelligentsia of the coastal districts on the West Coast, this passion for liberation must be understood as lying behind every industrial dispute, every political agitation. This is the true Africa. And that is why the whites fear them so much and seek to terrorize them. Dr. Buell wrote over ten years ago. Since then have taken place the Congo revolts already treated which had little or nothing to do with religion. Watch Tower, it should be noted, preaches a fierce resentment against all the imperialist Powers. It does not seek to distinguish between the Fascist and the democratic imperialisms. To the vast body of Africans in Africa such a distinction is meaningless.

The implications of this suppressed but burning resentment reach far. If, for instance, a revolt began in the Congo and spread to South Africa, East Africa, West Africa, the Africans could easily overwhelm the whites if these could no longer receive assistance from abroad. In Nigeria, with a population of twenty millions, there are less than 5,000 white people, and in Lagos, a town of 150,000 people, there are only 1,000 whites. There are many whites in South Africa, which forms a special problem, but the real basis of imperialist control in Africa is the cruisers and aeroplanes of Europe.

Though often retarded and sometimes diverted, the current of history, observed from an eminence, can be seen to unite strange and diverse tributaries in its own embracing logic. The San Domingo revolutionaries, the black arm in the Civil War, were unconscious but potent levers in two great propulsions forward of modern civilization. To-day the Rhodesian copper-miner, living the life of three shillings a week, is but another cog in the wheels of a creaking world economy, as uneconomic in the twentieth century as a naked slave in the cotton-fields of Alabama a hundred years ago. But Negro emancipation has expanded with the centuries;

what was local and national in San Domingo and America is to-day an international urgency, entangling the future of a hundred million Africans with all the hopes and fears of Western Europe. Though dimly, the political consciousness immanent in the historical process emerges in groping and neglected Africa. If Toussaint wrote in the language of '89, the grotesquerie of Watch Tower primitively approximates to the dialectic of Marx and Lenin. This it is which lifts out of bleakness and invests with meaning a record of failure almost unrelieved. The African bruises and breaks himself against his bars in the interest of freedoms wider than his own.

EPILOGUE

The History of Africa Revolt:
A Summary of 1939-1969.

I have to review the 30 years from 1938 when this book was published to 1969. This involves the social, using the word in the broadest sense, and the political activity, defeats and successes of hundreds of millions of people in Africa; tens of millions in the United States; and a few million in the West Indies who make up in intensity and potentiality for the insignificance of their numbers. Apart from the mere mass of the material, few periods in history exceed, in fact approach, the range of achievement, change, dramatic events and striking personalities of this particular period in history. Under these circumstances it is necessary even, at the cost of a few hundred words, where words are so precious, to make clear what can be done and what cannot be done, in fact to set the tone and the mood in which this review must be approached.

Anatole France (now alas low in critical estimation) made many not only witty but wise observations: A famous ruler, after many successes not excluding failures, called to-gether the wise men of his kingdom and told them he wanted them to study and report to him the facts and the understanding of History. The learned old men accepted the responsibility, gathered their assistants and their materials and retired for 20 years. They then returned with 20 volumes in which they had summarised the facts and the significance of History. By this time the monarch was an old man and he complained: How do you expect me at my age to cope with all that, to read far less to study 20 large volumes? Go away and summarise the 20 volumes so that I will be able to read them. The historians went away and after 20 years one very old man with a long beard returned with a single volume. Sire, he said, my fellow scholars are all dead. I have summarised it all and here it is in one volume. The monarch lay on what he knew to be his death bed, and he bitterly complained. You mean to say that I will never know the facts and the significance of History? How can I read even that large single volume which you bring to me? The old historian put the book aside and told him: Sire, I can summarize the history of man for you so that you can understand it before you die: They were born, they suffered, they died.

I wish my readers to understand the History of Negro Revolt during the last 30 years. They fought, they suffered, they are still fighting. Once we understand that we can then tackle our problems with the necessary mental equilibrium.

First Africa: I shall take only two of the nearly 50 African States which have won their independence or increased their powers. The first is what we know today as Ghana,

the second is Kenya. It helps that I have known personally
the national leaders of both countries.

I Africa
Gold Coast to Ghana

There lived in Accra a sub-chief called Nii Kwabena
Bonne III. He was also a business man. He made a short
campaign through the country enlisting the support of the
Chiefs. He then, on January 11, 1948, called a boycott on
the purchase of European imported goods. The boycott was
as complete as such an undertaking could be. It became
general in the Colony and Ashanti and lasted until the 24th
of February.

During the boycott events of immense symbolical significance took place. Native administrations, up to this point,
like the Chiefs, tools of the Government, now used their legal
position to impose fines upon those who did not cooperate in
the boycott of European goods. Groups of young men went
around the towns maintaining the boycott by force when
necessary.

It was only on the 11th of February that the Government
intervened. There was a series of meetings between the
Chamber of Commerce and Nii Bonne III, with the Colonial
Secretary in the Chair. It was agreed that prices should be
lowered for a trial period of three months. Nii Bonne III
then called off the boycott.

Meanwhile, the Ex-Servicemen's Union planned to present a petition to the Governor setting forth their grievances on Monday, the 24th of February, 1948, but they postponed it until Saturday, the 28th. On that day the Ex-Servicemen's Union began their march. In the course of it they changed the prescribed route and announced their determination to march on Christianborg Castle, the residence of the Governor. They found a squad of police in their way and in the course of the dispute which followed, the Superintendent of Police, a white man, fired at the ringleaders, killed two of them and wounded four or five. The news spread into the industrial district of Accra where the people for the first time in a month were buying European goods. They were already dissatisfied because they believed that the goods were not being sold to them at the prices stated in the published agreement which had preceded the calling off of the boycott. The news of the shooting precipitated an outburst of rage. The people attacked the European shops and looted them. The police were unable to restore order for two days, Saturday the 28th and Sunday the 29th. There was destruction of property by fire and in the two days 15 persons were killed and 115 injured in Accra alone: There were other disturbances in various parts of the Colony. The most important were at Koforidua where the outbreak began after the arrival of a lorry with men from Accra. They broke out in Kumasi

and district on Monday, March 1st, an hour after the arrival
of the train from Accra.

Nkrumah says that he and his organization, the United
Gold Coast Convention, had nothing whatever to do with the
disturbances, and, as we shall see, there is every reason to
believe him.

These are the bare facts of the case. When, however, we
look a little more closely in the light of after-events, an often-
analysed logical movement discloses itself. These were no
ordinary riots of a hungry populace over high prices. The
first stage of every revolution is marked by a great mass
movement of the populace, usually led by representatives of
the old order. M. Georges Lefevre of that great school of
historians, the French historians of the French Revolution,
has established that the bourgeois revolution in France in
1789 was preceded by what he calls the monarch which took
place in 1788, one year before the popular eruption which
captured the Bastille on July 14, 1789. In this case we are
in the middle of the Twentieth Century. The first outburst
takes the form of an economic boycott that lasted a month,
but it is led by a Chief and supported by the Chiefs. The
people of Accra follow exactly the course that the masses of
the people have followed in every great revolution. The
only organisation at hand was the organisation of ex-servicemen, and when they began their march they were at once
reinforced by large numbers of spectators and sympathisers.

Whatever had been the original intention of the ex-servicemen, these sympathisers encouraged them to take the road
to the Governor's Castle. Anti-racial cries were frequently
uttered. Among the remarks were such as "This is the last
European Governor who will occupy the Castle." (They
were not far wrong; he was the last but one.) The crowd
directed a heavy fusillade of stones against the police. When
the police tried to stop them, they shouted insults at the
European officers and invited the Africans in the ranks to
abandon their duty. It seems that they were successful. For
when the Superintendent finally gave the order to fire, the
Africans did not shoot and he himself had to seize a rifle
from the nearest man to fire the shots which caused the
casualties. Superintendent Imray had with him at the time
only ten men. The idea that a crowd of 2,000, many of them
men who had seen battle, was cowed by the shooting is
ridiculous. They could have swept the ten men away in ten
seconds, and as there was only two officers and 20 men at
Christianborg, the Castle could easily have become another
Bastille. In these situations you have to work by inferences,
similar conjunctures in previous historical situations and an
absence of prejudice against crowds and against Africans.
The crowd retreated because it realised that to sweep away
the petty resistance which faced it would be to initiate a
battle for which it knew was not prepared. Therefore, as

crowds will do under such circumstances, it preferred to
retreat.

I am here using the report of the investigations made
later by a Colonial Office Commission, and it must be remembered first that at moments like these what the crowd
is really thinking and the motives of its actions are profoundly difficult to recapture after the actions have taken
place; and in any case a Government Commission is not exactly the body which would know whom to question, how to
elicit the answers that matter, and even to understand what
evidence it does manage to collect. The Commission calls
the crowd a "lawless mob." That was precisely what it was
not. It was acting instinctively according to certain fundamental laws of revolution and we shall see that it obeys these
laws to the very end.

We should note these incipient actions carefully because, unless there is a great unsettlement of the settled
policy of His Majesty's Government and the other European
powers, that is precisely what is going to take place over vast
areas of colonial Africa. What has really taken place can be
summed up as follows:

1. The people on a national scale have mobilised and
organised themselves during the boycott and felt their power,
and they have been able to do so rapidly because this first
step is taken under their traditional leaders, their Chiefs.

2. The call to the African police not to obey their Eu-

ropean officers and not to shoot was not an accident. It takes place at the beginning of all revolutions. Neither was it spontaneous. Already, during the boycott, at the trial of a local chief on a charge arising out of the enforcement of the boycott, posters had appeared in Accra calling upon the police to strike and to refuse to obey the orders of the European officers.

3. The march on Christianborg Castle and the shouts that the Governor would be the last European governor show that out of the confidence built up in the month-long boycott, the people had proclaimed the ultimate slogan of the revolution, the end of imperial rule.

They know what they wanted. If they turned aside from the direct march to the Castle and hesitated before sweeping aside the police, it was because they understood the consequences of such actions. They had been waiting for somebody to lead them and they welcomed Nkrumah as a person to do so. Lawless mob indeed. Within 18 months Nkrumah was going to call a Ghana Constituent Assembly in Accra which would be attended by 90,000 people. Within two years these people would carry out a policy of Positive Action in which the life of the whole country would be brought to a standstill with the utmost discipline and order. Within three years they would give Nkrumah a vote of 22,780 out of a possible 23,122.

Nkrumah was taken out of jail to be made Leader of Government Business. Then after years of in-fighting he finally achieved the independence of the Gold Coast in 1957.

Myth of Mau Mau

Not African beliefs and tribal practices but land and white settlers on the land were to be decisive in shaping the character of the black revolt in Kenya. The railway made possible the export of cash crops by Europeans settled on the fertile temperate land of the Kenya Highlands. A policy of encouraging white settlement, a new policy in Africa, soon received the official blessing of the Foreign Office. Subsequently, under Colonial Office supervision, European settlement rapidly became the most powerful influence in the social, economic, and political development of the new country.

It was in the first decade of the twentieth century that this new Kenya took shape. One of the largest early applications for land (500 square miles) was made in April 1902 by the East Africa Syndicate, a company with a strong South African interest. With only a dozen settlers established at the beginning of 1903, in August the Commissioner, Sir Charles Eliot, sent his Collector of Customs, A. Marsden, to South Africa to encourage settlers to migrate to the country. By the end of 1905 over a million acres of land had been leased or sold by the Protectorate authorities. In 1906 a large party of Boer "Irreconcilables" trekked overland from the Transvaal to the Kenya highlands; others poured in by boat from Britain and South Africa.

Thus began something new in an African colony: the struggle to make it a "white man's country."

Nowhere in Africa was there such a struggle as began before 1914 and lasted decade after decade until it culminated in the independence of Kenya nearly fifty years later.

Between 1903 and 1906 important areas of Kikuyu land were alienated. Some 8,000 shillings was paid in compensation to 8,000 Kikuyu, but more than 3,000 received nothing at all. Commissioner Eliot was to write that "no one can doubt that the rich and exceptionally fertile district of Kikuyu is destined to be one of the chief centres of European cultivation, and the process of settlement is facilitated by the fact that there are gaps where there is no native population."

By 1914 the exclusive "White Highlands" was already a reality, and the Europeans were demanding the conventional right of British colonists to elect their own representatives to the Protecorate's Legislative Council.

The struggle was continuous. Ultimately (by the early fifties) the Africans, mainly but not entirely Kikuyu, took to arms, and from encampments and hiding places in the forests raided settled establishments and slew white farmers and those Africans who supported the British regime. Dedan

Kimathi and Waruhiu Itote ("General China") were gen-
erally acknowledged as the senior leaders of the nationalist
armies. Food, funds, arms, medical supplies could be secured
only by immense risks and labours. In some parts the Home
Guard was strong, in others week. In some areas the chief
was sympathetic, in others he was a dedicated "loyalist."
There were some wonderful leaders whose names ought to
be recorded—Kimathi himself, Stanley Mathenge, China, and
Tanganyika in Nyeri, Matenjagwo, Kago, and Mbaria Kaniu
in Fort Hall, and Kimbo, the cattle raider, operating between
Nanyuki and Maivasha. The difficult terraine prevented easy
lateral communication within the forest itself, and the campaign soon developed into a series of local battles of attrition,
ridge by ridge.

Though defeated in the Reserves, and with some sur-
rendering to the British Security Forces, nonetheless many
men and women in the forest continued their resistance.
Their aim, apart from surviving and carrying on the struggle
for land and freedom, was to attract international attention
to their cause. No outside help was forthcoming, and the
Emergency did not give rise to a major political investigating
commission from Britain.

From 1953 to 1955, Kimathi sought to provide an overall
perspective of the resistance in the forest. At one point, while
in the forest, Kimathi was reported to have said: "I do not
lead rebels but I lead Africans who want their self-govern-

ment and land. My people want to live in a better world than they met with when they were born. I lead them because God never created a true and real brotherhood between white and black so that we may be regarded as people and as human beings who can do each and everything."

Yet the plain fact is that the nationalist army in the forests was defeated by the huge forces sent by the British Government to maintain the colonial regime. Some 50,000 Kikuyu and other revolutionaries were detained in special camps to undergo special training to cure them of the mental disease which the British authorities discovered as the cause of their refusal to submit. Jomo Kenyatta was given a long prison sentence and, having served it, was confined far away from the centre of Kenya politics.

Despite this reconstitution of physical and military authority the British found that they could no longer govern the people of Kenya. Constitutional manipulation and constitutional manœuvre were worked out, agreed upon by the British Parliament and its experts, only to meet rejection and failure. In the end Kenya had to be granted political independence. The stories spread about "Mau Mau" have been exposed for the anti-African myths that they are. There is nothing inherently African about "Mau Mau." Their social organisation and corresponding beliefs being broken up and persecuted by the British, what was (by the British) labelled as Mau Mau was an ad hoc body of beliefs, oaths, disciplines newly created for the specific purpose of gathering and strengthening the struggle against British imperialism, its military, political and economic domination and, in particular, the Christianity it sought to inject and impose.

Independence and After

In the Gold Coast and in Kenya we have the two extremes of the African struggles for independence. Nothing in modern history was more startling than the rapidity with which other African states achieved political independence. In Algeria the French imperialists had an experience similar to the Kenya experience. The French military had established what they considered military power over the necessarily not well organised Algerian nationalist forces. They believed that they had established control over the political resistance. They engineered General de Gaulle into power in France in order finally to teach Algerians that they were French. But the General understood a revolutionary upheaval better than they did . He realised that whatever the strength of guns and of prisons, the colonial mentality of accepting domination was broken and could never be restored. To the fury of the French imperialists and army he worked out an independence agreement with the Algerian nationalists, saving what he could for French finance and capital. Such was the disappointment and anger of the

French generals in particular that they tried to assassinate him. So blatant was their attempt that some of them had to be tried and even jailed. Such was the naked proof of the rapacity of that small section of the population of an advanced civilisation which profited by imperialism. Similarly, thousands of Frenchmen who had lived well by exploiting the Algerian people left Algeria and returned to France.

The murder of Lumumba and the tireless efforts of the late Tshombe dramatised the attempt by Belgian imperialism to maintain its exploitation of the vast mineral wealth of the Congo, while giving some token recognition to the irresistable movement for national independence.

The dozen years that have unfolded since the winning of independence by the Gold Coast in 1957 are some of the most far-ranging and politically intense that history has known. African state after African state has gained political independence with a tumultous rush that was not envisaged, even by the most sanguine of the early advocates of independence. The names of leaders obscure the political reality. What is to be noted is that Kenyatta, Nkrumah, Banda, to take the best-known names, were all imprisoned by the British Government and *had to be released to head the independent states*. The British Government, as did the French and Belgian, found that despite their soldiers, their guns and planes, they could not rule. The colonial mentality having been broken, the only way to restore some sort of order or, to reject a word now corrupted and offensive, the only way to have a viable society was to transfer the man in jail to be the head of state. In no other way could the African people once more accommodate themselves to any social structure.

They accepted the African leader and his African colleagues. But that is precisely why in African state after African state, with almost the rapidity with which independence was gained, military dictatorship after military dictatorship has succeeded to power, the most depressing of all being the overthrow of what had appeared to be the most progressive and successful of the new African governments— the government of Mali. What are the reasons for this rapid decay and decline of African nationalism? The best known and the reason most often advanced by Africans and advocates of African independence is the continued exploitation by the industrial and finance-capital of Europe and the United States. Even people no more than casually informed are aware of the continual lowering of the prices of the commodities, most often single-crop or unit-minerals, produced by the African countries, and the raising of the prices of the manufactured goods needed by the newly independent African countries in their necessarily frantic efforts to modernise themselves. Banks, and old industries with new African names working through local agents (such as the East Indian community in Kenya) continue to control the life of the newly independent African communities. "Aid," so small in quantity and so large in publicity, would gladly be dispensed with, if economic independence were automatically to result from political independence.

However, without minimising the continuing economic subordination of the newly independent African states, there are objective reasons for the apparent decline, in fact abrupt disintegration and resort to crude military dictatorship in African state after African state.

The States which the African nationalist leaders inherited were not in any sense African. With the disintegration of the political power of the imperialist states in Africa and the rise of militancy of the African masses, a certain political pattern took shape. Nationalist political leaders built a following, they or their opponents gained support among the African civil servants who had administered the imperialist state, and the newly independent African state was little more than the old imperialist state only now administered and controlled by black nationalists. That these men, western-educated and western-oriented, had or would have little that was nationalist or African to contribute to the establishment of a truly new and truly African order was seen most clearly by the late Frantz Fanon, and he established his still constantly increasing reputation by his untrammelled advocacy of revolt against these black nationalist regimes. Uncompromising revolt he saw as the only means of ridding Africa of the economic and psychological domina-

tion by Western civilisation which, independence or no independence, seemed certain to keep Africa and Africans hewers
of wood and drawers of water to Western Civilisation. Sekou
Tour of Guinea seemed to be the only African leader who
aimed at building a society which would use European
techniques to strengthen and develop the African heritage.
But not only was Guinea a very small and very underdeveloped state, but the Moscow assistants whom he hoped would
help him, plotted to overthrow his regime and Guinea did not
make the progress which would set an example for Africa.
That example, however, was to come from Tanzania, under
the leadership of Dr. Nyerere. The impact that the policies
of Tanzania has made upon Africa and can in time make
upon the rest of the world, underdeveloped or advanced, has
already established the African state of Tanzania as one of
the foremost political phenomena of the twentieth century.
Tanzania is the highest peak reached so far by revolting
blacks and it is imperative to make clear, not least of all to
blacks everywhere, the new stage of political thought which
has been reached. But first to establish some idea of what
is happening in other areas of Negro political reality and
response since 1938.

II SOUTH AFRICA

Since the end of World War II nowhere has any regime
in the world (or for that matter any modern historical re-

gime) made it more clear what is its primary and permanent concern. This preoccupation is the repression and containment of the increasing revolutionary rejection of its exploitation and oppression by the millions of blacks on whose backs it lives and thrives. Such is the record which the South African regime of whites daily registers in contemporary history aided by the benevolent neutrality of Europe and America, and the border states that it seeks to build and strengthen against political destruction by a self-conscious independent African continent.

All that will be attempted here is to give what is usually neglected, the pressure, the objective social pressures which the South African blacks, the most highly developed in Africa, exercise on the very vitals of the South African regime.

A Prime Minister of South Africa, Mr. B. J. Vorster, made it absolutely clear that the regime had no intention of giving political rights to urban Africans. Speaking in Parliament on April 24, 1968, he said:

> . . . They remain there because they cannot provide employment for themselves. But the fact that you employ those people, does not place you under any obligation to grant them political rights in your parliament. Surely the fact that you work for a man does not give you the right to run his affairs? . . . It is true that there are Blacks working for us. They will continue to work for us for genera-

tions, in spite of the ideal we have to separate them completely·. . . .

The fact of the matter is this; we need them, because they work for us, but, after all, we pay them for their work . . . But the fact that they work for us can never . . . entitle them to claim political rights. Not now, nor in the future . . . under no circumstances can we grant them those political rights in our own territory, neither now nor never."

That indicates the fear that white South Africa has of the blacks.

Any examination of South Africa's labour laws and policies will show the pretence and the reality of the status of Africans in the urban areas. More than 4,000,000 Africans live in the urban areas. In spite of desperate measures to limit the flow of Africans into the towns, the urban African population doubled between 1945 and 1960, when 3,471,233 were counted in the census. For twelve of those remarkable 15 years, the Nationalist government was busily engaged in applying its policy of keeping the races apart.

For better appreciation of the situation, one should study the racial composition of the 13 principal urban areas, listed in the accompanying table. These centres of industrial and commercial activity have been designated "white" areas, although their white population is far less than their non-white.

The greatest concentration of industry is on the Witwatersrand, where there are twice as many non-whites as whites and Africans alone outnumber whites by over half-a-million.

POPULATION OF PRINCIPAL URBAN AREAS 1960 (APPROXIMATE)

	Africans	Whites	Coloureds	Asians
Johannesburg	650,912	413,153	59,467	28,993
Cape Town	75,200	305,155	417,881	8,975
Durban	221,535	196,398	27,082	236,477

The purpose of the Urban Areas Act is to control the influx of Africans into the urban areas; to set apart areas for their accommodation; to direct their labour; and to impose strict regulations for their control and movement. In short, it aims at providing whites with black labour without allowing blacks to acquire residential, social and other rights in the areas where they are employed. Try as they will, the South African whites cannot isolate or circumscribe the black population. The simple truth is that without the participation of the black population the South African economy would fall apart.

Here are some figures, published by the Anti-Apartheid Movement in February 1969.

POPULATION (mid-1967)	Numbers	Percentage
Africans	12¾ million	68%
Whites	3½ million	19%
Coloureds	1¾ million	10%
Indians	½ million	3%
	18¾ million	100%

88% of the Coloured people live in the Cape.

83% of the Indian people live in Natal. They are debarred from living on the Orange Free State.

Distribution of population by race in each of the four largest cities (per cent):

	Whites	Africans	Coloureds	Indians
Johannesburg	36	56	5	3
Cape Town	38	9	52	1
Durban	29	32	4	35
Pretoria	49	47	2	2

There have been created three so-called African states, Transkei, Ciskei and Tswanaland, labelled Bantustans so as to create some sense of race and nation separate from white South Africa. That cannot alter nor mitigate the remorseless pressures of the blacks of South Africa against the whites. The imprisonings, the tortures and the shootings now have been met by guerilla warfare substantially authenticated.

One thing is certain. The existing regime in South Africa can continue to exist only by the increasing persecution and brutal repression of the existing blacks. History in general, and the particulars of this history, indicate a violent end to this regime sooner or later, and sooner rather than later.

III *The United States*

1952 was the first year in 71 years that there were no lynchings. But that does not mean that the bodies of black men who had offended whites were no longer found floating in shallow waters, or that at times black men disappeared, their relations and friends uncertain whether they had gone North or had been liquidated by white racists. The National Association for the Advancement of Coloured People, a predominantly middle-class organization, chiefly of blacks but including sympathetic whites, concentrated on the abolition of legal discrimination against Negroes and earned notable successes. Legal struggles and mass action reacted on each other. The famous bus boycott in Montgomery, Alabama, began on December 5, 1955, and this action, of a range and solidity unprecedented, unloosed a flood which became a torrent. On 5 June 1956 a Federal court ruled that racial segregation on Montgomery city buses violated the Constitution. Later that year, the Supreme Court upheld a lower court decision which banned segregation on Montgomery buses. Federal injunctions prohibiting this segregation were served on city, state and bus company officials on December 20. At mass meetings, Montgomery blacks called off the year-long bus boycott, and buses were integrated on December 21.

Congress passed the Civil Rights Act of 1957, the first federal civil rights legislation since 1875. That very year, President Eisenhower, with obvious reluctance to take such a step, ordered federal troops to Little Rock, Arkansas, to prevent interference with school integration at Central High School. That was on September 24. These episodes might have seemed to be merely unusual types of struggles which in the past had been half-heartedly projected or even attempted. Rapidly they showed themselves to be precipitants of the greatest social crisis the United States had known since the Civil War.

It was black students who initiated this struggle. On February 1, 1960 four students from a North Carolina college started a sit-in movement at Greensboro, North Carolina, in a five and dime store. By February 10 the movement had spread to fifteen Southern cities in five states. In March, one thousand Alabama state students marched on the State Capitol and held a protest meeting. In April the Student Nonviolent Coordinating Committee was organised on the Shaw University campus. In May, President Eisenhower signed the Civil Rights Act of 1960, but that was insignificant in comparison with the tremendous movement that now began among blacks: the masses of the population in city after city; the groups of "Freedom Riders"—black young men and women who faced the bombs, bullets, whips and prisons of the South, official and unofficial; the black students on the campuses; black youths in the schools. Let it not be forgotten that both the New Left and the revolutionary defiance of campus authority by white students began to take shape as a direct result of the black students turning from protests by asking for reforms to protests by revolutionary action.

It would be a mistake here to attempt to give details about either events or personalities. Even to name some is to omit and thereby discriminate against others. It may be said, however, that names such as Leroi Jones, Stokely Carmichael, Eldridge Cleaver, Rap Brown, Malcolm X, Martin Luther King, the Black Panthers, are household names not only among young people in the United States but among white populations all over the world. Summer after summer has seen tremendous struggles by the black masses, led by unknown, obscure, local leaders. Perhaps the most significant was that which followed the assassination of Dr. Martin Luther King, the world-famous black leader. The American government placed a cordon of troops around the White House and government buildings and areas in Washington. They then abandoned the city, the capital of the United States, to the embittered and insurgent blacks, who constitute a majority of the Washington population. The question to be asked: what else could the government have done?

One can only record the question most often and most seriously asked: can any government mobilise the white population, or a great majority of it, in defence of white racism against militant blacks? The only legitimate answer lies in the continuing militancy or retreat of the black population. This population is at least 30 million in number strategically situated in the heart of many of the most important cities in the United States. If the black population continues to resist racism, the militants and youth actively and the middle classes sympathetic or neutral, then the physical defeat of the black struggle against racism will involve the destruction of the United States as it has held together since 1776.

IV *The Caribbean*

The Caribbean is a small area where British and French have ruled for centuries and where at the present one or two British territories have been granted what is known as independence. There are a few points that are to be made about these extraordinarily significant but on the world scale minute territories.

First of all, it is only recently that a British scholar, Sir Richard Pares, in a work called *Merchants and Planters* has made it clear that as far back as the middle of the eighteenth

century the slaves actually ran the plantations, those plantations that were the source of so much wealth, which contributed so substantially to the advancement of the advanced
countries. *Merchants and Planters* is a study of the Caribbean and was published for the Economic History Society
at the Cambridge University Press. Pares notes that:

> . . . in all the inventories which are to be found among the
> West Indian archives it is very usual for the mill, the
> cauldron, the still and the buildings to count for more than
> one-sixth of the total capital; in most plantations one-
> tenth would be nearer the mark. By far the greatest capital
> items were the value of the slaves and the acreage planted
> in canes by their previous labour.

So that the greatest capital value (about 1760) of the
sugar plantations, was the labour of the slaves and the acres
they had planted. All sorts of economists do all sorts of
studies about the West Indies but they don't know that the
real value of those precious economic units was the slaves
and the land they had developed by their labours, this escapes nearly all except this English scholar.

Pares goes on to say:

> Yet, when we look closely, we find that the industrial
> capital required was much larger than a sixth of the total
> value. With the mill, the boiling house and the still went
> an army of specialists—almost all of them slaves, but none
> the less specialists for that.

There was an army of slaves, but they were specialists. This tremendous economy that made so much wealth particularly for British society—it was the slaves who ran those plantations. Pares drives home the point:

> They were not only numerous but, because of their skill, they had a high value. If we add their cost to that of the instruments and machinery which they used, we find that the industrial capital of the plantations without which it could not be a plantation at all, was probably not much less than half its total capital.

Pares obviously feels it imperative to reiterate what he no doubt has failed to find in previous studies.

> . . . but when we examine specifications of the negroes, we find so many boilers, masons, carters, boatswains of the mill, etc., that we cannot feel much confidence in our categories, especially when we find individuals described as "excellent boiler and field negro" . . .

So that about 1766 Negroes ran the plantations. A man is described as an excellent boiler and field Negro, but this prevents us from putting such persons on either side of the line. He not only worked in the fields but also did the necessary technical work. Further complication arises from the fact that specialist jobs were awarded to the sickly and the ruptured. The sickly or the ruptured were given the technical jobs to do—we have to look afresh at the rapid spread of technical skill.

That gives an entirely different picture of the kind of civilisation that was in existence in the West Indies well before the French Revolution of 1789. In the United States in general skilled labour was the preserve of whites. There were no white labours in the Caribbean. There is other evidence elsewhere and it seems legitimate to say that the slaves ran the society. If they had been removed the society would have collapsed. That in fact is perfectly clear in certain writings about Trinidad and Tobago.

This is the process whereby the inhabitants of these Caribbean Islands have made an astonishing mastery of the techniques of Western civilisation. Race prejudice, however, continues to be subtly, and not so subtly, a dominant feature of the social structure of the islands. What has happened is that the population, without any native background (the Amerindians were all wiped out), have been compelled to master the languages and the techniques of Western civilisation which they have done with astonishing skill. The struggle for African and black independence is studded with distinguished individuals of Caribbean origin: René Maran, winner of the Prix Concourt in 1921 for his exposure in his novel *Batouala* of French degradation of the African peoples in Africa, where he worked as a civil servant; Marcus Garvey, George Padmore, Frantz Fanon, Aimé Cesairé, Stokely Carmichael. . . . But this mastery of certain aspects of Western civilisation has been able to exercise itself fully only in

Western Europe and the United States for the imperialist powers continue, as they have done from the beginning, to dominate the economic and finances of the territories. The only difference today is that black men administer the imperialist interests. The situation is highly explosive. Whereas the economy continues to be a colonialist economy of the seventeenth century, completely dominated by foreign powers, the population is a modern population, a population of the twentieth century, learned in the langues and techniques of Western civilisation and highly developed because of the smallness of the islands and the close relations between what is technically known as urban and rural. A federation was attempted in the British islands, the British being anxious to rid themselves of the responsibility of these islands, the Caribbean being now an American sea. But the federation fell apart. The reason is very simple: A federation meant that the economic line of direction should no longer be from each island to London, previously the financial and economic capital of each territory. The new lines of direction should have been from island to island. But this involved the break-up of the old colonial system. The West Indian politicians preferred the break-up of the federation.

What is the situation in the islands, what is inherent there and what may break out at any minute, is proved by the revolt that has in 1969 broken out in the island of Curacao dominated by Dutch oil interests.

The revolt was a revolt of workers and unemployed youth and they burned down business houses of a value variously estimated between 15 and 40 millions (Dutch money). On the surface the revolt was a spontaneous process against Westcar, a sub-contractor of Shell Oil, who lowered salaries and laid off workers. But the ensuing strike spread to Shell, representing more than 90% of the national income. The workers marched on Parliament and when the marchers clashed with a column of armed police the eruption broke out.

Meanwhile, 300 political prisoners are in the penitentiary. According to local law, they can be kept there if need be for two years while their cases are being investigated.

Nominally "peace" would have been achieved by the arrival of 600 Dutch marines, but not in 1969. An uneasy peace was really secured by the resignation of the Democratic Government which had been in power for 14 years. Facing a Revolution, it has agreed to hold elections. It is freely stated by leaders of the Working Class Front that if the Democratic Government is re-elected, the events of May will be repeated with even greater devastation.

Herbert Specer, President of the Federation of Petroleum Workers, states what is the obvious truth:

> In the last analysis the significance of the May revolt is that people want change, and if they don't get it anything could happen.

Small as they are, their historical origin and development have been such that these Caribbean islands can make highly significant contributions to the economics and politics of a world in torment. That is exactly what Castro's Cuba has done.

V ". . . Always Out of Africa"

For many hundreds of years, in fact almost (though not quite) from the beginning of the contact between Western civilisation and Africa, it has been the almost universal practice to treat African achievement, discoveries and creations as if Western civilisation was the norm and the African people spent their years in imitating, trying to reach or, worse still, if necessary going through the primitive early stages of the Western world. We therefore will, before we place it historically, state as straightforwardly as possible the historical achievements that are taking place today in an African state.

First the Tanzanian Government has nationalised the chief centres of economic life in the territory. That though important and necessary is not sufficient to create a new society. Less and less is nationalisation becoming a landmark of a new society—today right-wing military dictators (Peru) and the Catholic hierarchy (with the blessing of the Pope) are ready to nationalise and even confiscate. The Government of Tanzania has gone further. In the Arusha Declaration of 29 January 1967 it aims at creating a new type of government official:

PART FIVE

THE ARUSHA RESOLUTION

Therefore, the National Executive Committee, meeting in the Community Centre at Arusha from 26.1.67 to 29.1.67, resolves:

A. *The Leadership*

1. Every TANU and Government leader must be either a Peasant or a Worker, and should in no way be associated with the practices of Capitalism or Feudalism.
2. No TANU or Government leader should hold shares in any company.
3. No TANU or Government leader should hold Directorship in any privately-owned enterprises.
4. No TANU or Government leader should receive two or more salaries.
5. No TANU or Government leader should own houses which he rents to others.
6. For the purposes of this Resolution the term "leader" should comprise the following: Members of the TANU National Executive Committee; Ministers, Members of Parliament, Senior Officials of Organisations affiliated to TANU, Senior Officials of Para-Statal Organisations, all those appointed or elected under any clause of the TANU Constitution, Councillors, and Civil Servants in high and middle cadres. (In this context "leader" means a man, or a man and his wife; a woman, or a woman and her husband).

Such a resolution would probably exclude 90 percent of those who govern and administer in other parts of the world, developed or under-developed. The Government aims at creating a new type of society, based not on Western theories but on the concrete circumstances of African life and its historic past.

Perhaps the most revolutionary change of all, it will reconstruct the very system of education in order to fit the children and the youth, *in particular the youth in secondary education,* for the new society which the Government of Tanzania seeks to build. The simplicity with which Dr. Nyerere states what his government proposes to do disguises the fact that not in Plato or Aristotle, Rousseau or Karl Marx will you find such radical, such revolutionary departures from the established educational order.

> Alongside this change in the approach to the curriculum there must be a parallel and integrated change in the way our schools are run, so as to make them and their inhabitants a real part of our society and our economy. Schools must, in fact, become communities—and communities which practise the precept of self-reliance. The teachers, workers, and pupils together must be the members of a social unit in the same way as parents, relatives, and children are the family social unit. There must be the same kind of relationship between pupils and teachers within the school community as there is between children and parents in the village. And the former community must realise, just as the latter do, that their life and well-being

depend upon the production of wealth—by farming or other activities.

This means that all schools, but especially secondary schools and other forms of higher education, must contribute to their own upkeep; they must be economic communities as well as social and educational communities. Each school should have, as an integral part of it, a farm or workshop which provides the food eaten by the community, and makes some contribution to the total national income.

This is not a suggestion that a school farm or workshop should be attached to every school for training purposes. It is a suggestion that every school should also be a farm; that the school community should consist of people who are both teachers and farmers, and pupils and farmers. Obviously, if there is a school farm, the pupils working on it should be learning the techniques and tasks of farming. But the farm would be an integral part of the school— and the welfare of the pupils would depend on its output, just as the welfare of a farmer depends on the output of his land. Thus, when this scheme is in operation, the revenue side of school accounts would not just read as at present—"Grant from Government . . .; Grant from voluntary agency or other charity . . ." They would read— "Income from sale of cotton (or whatever other cash crop was appropriate for the area) . . .; Value of the food grown and consumed . . .; Value of labour done by pupils on new building, repairs, equipment, etc. . . .; Government subvention . . .; Grant from . . ."

Perhaps nothing shows more clearly the radical, the revolutionary, the complete break with Western habits and

Western thought than the new attitude to the Tanzanian farmer. Some of them have followed the advice given to the African farmer officially and unofficially by Westerners: wishing him and his country well, they have encouraged him to individual effort, essentially capitalistic. Following this advice farmers in certain districts of Tanzania (mainly the slopes of the Kavirondo Mountain) have followed this Western type of agriculture with success. Note now the economic, in fact the political attitude of the Tanzanian Government to this type of farmer. Reviewing Tanzania "After the Arusha Declaration" Dr. Nyerere outlines the co-operative socialist community Tanzania aims at. He continues:

> This is the objective. It is stated clearly, and at greater length, in the policy paper. We must understand it so that we know what we are working towards. But it is not something we shall achieve overnight. We have a long way to go.
>
> For what has been happening over recent years is quite different. We have not been enlarging and modernising our traditional family unit as much as abandoning it in favour of small-scale capitalist farming. Many of our most dynamic and energetic farmers, especially those with the most initiative and willingness to learn new techniques, have been branching out on their own as individuals. They have not been enlarging their farms by joining with others in a spirit of equality, but by employing labour. So we are getting the beginnings of the development of an agricultural labouring class on the one hand, and a wealthier employing class on the other. Fortunately, this develop-

ment has not gone very far; we can arrest the trend without difficulty. But we must not make this change by
persecuting the progressive farmers; after all, we have been
encouraging them in the direction they have been going!
Instead we must seek their cooperation, and integrate them
into the new socialist agriculture by showing them that
their best interests will be served by this development.
For energy and initiative such as these farmers have displayed will be very important to our progress. We need
these people.

This is something new in the history of political thought.
The co-operative villages aimed at are called UJAMAA and
Dr. Nyerere has called the whole new attempt to create a
new society Socialism. In our view he is entitled to do so,
and a proper respect for what the Tanzanian Government is
doing demands that it be related to traditional and contemporary concepts of socialism.

First of all, no one today believes that what exists in
Russia and Eastern Europe is, in any sense of the word,
socialist; that is to say, a society having achieved and aiming
at even more comprehensive stages of liberty, equality and
fraternity, social relations higher than those achieved by the
most advanced parliamentary democracy. That is socialism
or it is worse even than capitalist decay being then a deliberate and conscious fraud. Worse still, most unfortunately,
certain of the new African states, anxious to rid themselves
of the capitalist stigma, have invented a new category

labelled African socialism. Worthy of repetition is the exposition of this African socialism by one newly independent state.

Adaptability

15. African Socialism must be flexible because the problems it will confront and the incomes and desires of the people will change over time, often quickly and substantially. A rigid, doctrinaire system will have little chance for survival. The system must—

(i) make progress towards ultimate objectives; and

(ii) solve more immediate problems with efficiency.

16. No matter how pressing immediate problems may be, progress toward ultimate objectives will be the major consideration. In particular, political equality, social justice and human dignity will not be sacrificed to achieve more material ends more quickly. Nor will these objectives be comprised today in the faint hope that by so doing they can be reinstated more fully in some unknown and far distant future.

Whenever was there a state, beginning with the state of Adam and Eve, that did not, could not, proclaim that it had in mind ultimate objectives while paying attention to immediate needs? That is not socialism. It is nonsense. It is not African. It is bureaucratic balderdash, to which we are by now well accustomed in advanced as well as in underdeveloped fakers—a bold attempt by newcomers to dress the old reality in new clothes.

Far more important than this fakery is the recognition by President Kaunda of Zambia that the attempt merely to ape European ways, which has brought such wide fields of disaster to Africa, must not only be rejected but that there are new African paths to be explored. In his significantly named "Humanism in Zambia" President Kaunda says:

> This is a key point, for if the distribution of wealth is not done properly, it might lead to the creation of classes in society and the much-valued humanist approach that is traditional and inherent in our African society would have suffered a final blow. If this happened the world as a whole, and African in particular, would be all the poorer for it. For you would then have the "haves" and the "haves-nots". Politically you would be creating room for opposing parties based on "the oppressed" and "the oppressor" concept which again would not be in keeping with the society described above; a society in which the Chief as an elected or appointed leader of the people held national property like land in trust for the people, and he was fully aware that he was responsible to them. He knew, too, that his continuing to be their head depended on his people's will.

President Kaunda wants to show how important it is for Africans to break cleanly with the ideas of European well-wishers, that African progress depends on educating first a small number of Africans and then an increasing number who will gradually (without undue haste) educate more and more African natives to capitalist energies and the moderate

mastery of parliamentary democracy. His rejection of this
concept is total.

> Now we must ask again what effects will persistently in-
> creasing levels of specialisation have on our much valued
> traditional society in our country. This field of specialisa-
> tion drives people to resort to new groups in society. In
> other words, people with common interests group together,
> partly because of the community of their interests and
> partly as the means of promoting and protecting the wel-
> fare of their group. For example, a carpenter will find his
> own interests are not the same as those of the commercial
> farmer. The teacher finds that his interests differ from
> those of the mineworker. And so the whole list of differ-
> ent interests can be outlined. This point is, all this gives
> birth to a new disintegrative tendency. This, as can be
> seen, cuts right across the traditional society which has
> been described above as a mutual aid society which was
> an accepting and inclusive community.

Despite the low-level of economic development in
African states, this new African conception of the future of
Africa lays claim not only to a future, but also to deep roots
in the past.

President Kaunda insists on this:

> The traditional community was a mutual aid society. It
> was organised to satisfy the basic human needs of all its
> members and, therefore, individualism was discouraged.
> Most resources, such as land, might be communally owned
> and administered by chiefs and village headmen for the

benefit of everyone. If, for example, a villager required a
new hut, all the men would turn to forests and fetch poles
to erect the frame and bring grass for thatching. The
women might be responsible for making the mud-plaster
for the walls and two or three of them would undoubtedly
brew some beer so that all the workers would be refreshed
after a hot but satisfying day's work. In the same spirit,
the able-bodied would accept responsibility for tending
and harvesting the gardens of the sick and infirm.

This new recognition so characteristic first of Tanzania
and now of Zambia does not turn its back on the modernisa-
tion necessary in the modern world. Once more let the
African President speak:

> From what has been said above, it is clear that we cannot
> ourselves expect to achieve once again the Man-centred
> society without very careful planning. And in this direc-
> tion nothing is more important than institutions of
> learning . . .

Here the model is or will have to be that so clearly
delineated by Dr. Nyerere.

That is the essence of the matter. And the newly independent African states are in such crises that success in
Tanzania and real strides forward in hard-pressed Zambia
can initiate a new road for Africa—the mobilisation of the
African people to build an African society in an African way.

It would be a great mistake not to make clear how
closely this profoundly creative response to the African

reality corresponds with and indeed carries further the highest stages so far reached by Western political thought. Lenin had no illusions about the Russian Revolution. He knew that socialism in the Marxist sense was impossible in the Russia he knew, and in 1923 was leaving behind. In the last days he increasingly drew attention to two important aspects and needs of the Russia which he insisted on calling Socialist Russia, despite the fact that the great majority of the Russian population consisted of illiterate peasants. The Soviet State, he insisted in those last days, was not new. Behind the Marxist terminology and proletarian window dressing was the same old Tsarist state, not even a bourgeois state but a "bureaucratic-serf state." His proposals to alter these we need not go into. It is sufficient to know that Dr. Nyerere has seen through the reactionary, bureaucratic colonialist state which he inherited, and has gone further than anyone in the determination to break it up and make a new type of state.

Lenin also knew, none better, that the Soviet official had to leave high-flown theorising and personally go to work among the backward Russian peasants. In perhaps the most moving of his many statements of what the people needed from the Marxist officials of the Government, he says:

> Less Argument about words! We still have too much of this sort of thing. More variety in practical experience and more study of this experience! Under certain conditions

the exemplary organisation of local work, even on a small
scale, is of far greater national importance than many
branches of the central state work. And these are precisely
the conditions we are in at the present moment in regard
to peasant farming in general, and in regard to the exchange of the surplus products of agriculture for the manu-
factures of industry in particular. Exemplary organisation
in this respect, even in a single volost, is of far greater
national importance than the "exemplary" improvement of
the central apparatus of any People's Commissariat; for
three and a half years to such an extent that it has managed to acquire a certain amount of harmful inertness; we
cannot improve it quickly to any extent, we do not know
how to do it. Assistance in the more radical improvement
of it, a new flow of fresh forces, assistance in the successful
struggle against bureaucracy, in the struggle to overcome
this harmful inertness, must come from the localities, from
the lower ranks, with the exemplary organisation of a small
"whole", precisely a "whole", i.e., not one farm, not one
branch of economy, not one enterprise, but the *sum total*
of economic exchange, even if only in a small locality.
Those of us who are doomed to remain on work at the
centre will continue the task of improving the apparatus
and purging it of bureaucracy, even if in modest and immediately achievable dimensions. But the greatest assistance in this task is coming, and will come, from the
localicites . . .

Note in particular one of his last sentences: "We who
are doomed . . ." Lenin wanted to go and work among the
peasants. The great Marxist would have understood the profoundly socialist and human conception which has moved

Dr. Nyerere to break to pieces the old system of education and substitute a genuinely socialist and humanist procedure for the youth of Tanzania. In a conversation with Dr. Nyerere, the present writer (having previously read his writings) drew his attention to this particular passage from Lenin and what Lenin was striving to teach as far back as 1923. The African leader said that he did not know it—he had arrived at his conclusion by himself and with his people.

It is sufficient to say that socialist thought has seen nothing like this since the death of Lenin in 1924, and its depth, range and the repercussions which flow from it, go far beyond the Africa which gave it birth. It can fertilise and reawaken the mortuary that is socialist theory and practice in the advanced countries. "Marxism is a Humanism" is the exact reverse of the truth. The African builders of a humanist society show that today all humanism finds itself in close harmony with the original conceptions and aims of Marxism.

INDEX